Ge...

The Teach Yourself series has been trusted around the world
for over 60 years. This series of 'In A Week' business books is
designed to help people at all levels and around the world to
further their careers. Learn, in a week, what the experts learn

Geoff Ribbens MA, BSc, FCIPD has lectured on organizational behaviour to postgraduate management students, as well as carrying out consultancy and training. More recently, he has been business development coach for Oxford Innovation Ltd. Geoff became interested in non-verbal communication after several clients wanted him to explore how 'body language' influenced their management effectiveness and, indirectly, their business success.

Richard Thompson PhD is a writer, broadcaster and communications specialist with a background in the social sciences. He is the author of several books on stress management, life skills and self-help, focusing on conflict resolution in public and private life. His interest in body language was sparked by Geoff Ribbens' pioneering work on managerial effectiveness through enhanced recognition of non-verbal communication.

Body Language For Management

Geoff Ribbens
and
Richard Thompson

www.inaweek.co.uk

Hodder Education

338 Euston Road, London NW1 3BH.

Hodder Education is an Hachette UK company

First published in UK 2000 by Hodder Education

This edition published 2012.

Previous editions of this book were published by Hodder in 2000 and 2002

Also available in ebook

Contents

Introduction

Actions speak louder than words: a *thoughtful nod*, **a** *telling sigh*, **a** *studied gaze*, **a** *knowing smile*, *crossed arms*, **even the way you** *touch your nose*; **these are just a few of the hundreds of clues your body language gives away all the time, and yet you may not even be aware that it is happening.**

We take body language for granted because most of the time we are not conscious of it. Yet we use it to convey all kinds of messages and meanings – to emphasize, inform, suggest and even manipulate. Some of us are better at 'reading' it than others. That's because the more aware you are of how the body 'talks', the less you need to say and the more quickly you identify people's intentions, motives and attitudes.

We call this managing without words. As a manager, understanding body language helps you to communicate more effectively and to defuse conflict by enabling you to *look beyond what people say to what they really mean*. It's only when we look more closely that we begin to reveal things about ourselves and others that are so easily missed in the course of our busy working lives.

Much research carried out over the past few decades – in strangely named disciplines like paralinguistics, proxemics, chronemics, kinesics and neuro-linguistic programming – have helped to revolutionize our understanding of non-verbal communication. Rather like looking at the stars through a telescope for the first time, the research has revealed things we missed with the naked eye – adding definition and meaning to what we previously took for granted.

When applied to management, the ability to understand people's body language makes you not only a better active listener but also a more effective communicator and leader. Successful management depends upon positive leadership. Without it you have little more than the exercise of power.

People get where they are because they adopt different strategies for increasing their authority over others. Some are coercive, others manipulative, but such uses of power can be self-defeating as they destroy motivation and loyalty. It is those who maintain the right balance between assertiveness and self-awareness who climb the ladder to success.

Ultimately, success is as much about being seen to do your job well as actually doing it well. It's a simple fact of life that conveying the right impression can make up for deficiencies in knowledge and skills. Many talented managers fail to gain promotion because they make the mistake of thinking that success is judged on the basis of *what* they do well, rather than the *impression* they create in doing it.

Simply being aware of how people function isn't the same as demonstrating your willingness to listen or to connect with their needs. This book will show you how to understand body language as a first step towards being a better communicator. Applying these skills effectively will make you a more confident, self-assured and respected manager of people.

Geoff Ribbens and Richard Thompson

SUNDAY

Managing
without
words

Being a success in management isn't about winning or losing. It's about how you interact with others and gain their respect. Personal authority is built on trust, not fear, and the best managers are those who listen, not those who dictate or bully. Understanding body language enables us to 'tune into' the thoughts and feelings of colleagues, making them – and us – better at our jobs. By improving our communication skills we encourage others to perform at a higher level.

Language doesn't have to be in the form of words to make a point or grasp someone's meaning. The body 'talks' without the need for words through giveaway signs and signals that *add emphasis*, *suggest feelings* and *convey opinion* – just like punctuation on a page. It's when we miss these unspoken clues that we are open to deception. Learning to read the signs is like detective work: the better you are at it, the quicker you get to the truth.

Today you'll learn that body language skills aren't rocket science but a combination of common sense, accurate observation, intuition, reflection and application – adding meaning to what we previously took for granted. Once you have them, you'll never look back.

Body talk

It may surprise you to learn that less than 10 per cent of the meaning of what we communicate face to face is in the form of words. Although it is hard to believe, according to the findings of research into body language, **tone of voice** accounts for nearly 40 per cent of our meaning, and posture and gesture 50 per cent.

The point is that language is concerned with the expression of thoughts, ideas and feelings and its function is to enable communication to take place. **It doesn't have to be in the form of words** providing that we understand the message and grasp the meaning of what is being conveyed.

Body language does precisely this. By means of non-verbal communication we can convey what we think, how we feel and what we want through physical posture, gestures, facial expression, tone and strength of voice, even non-verbal sounds like grunts and sighs. Because we subconsciously use this language in our dealings with others, we tend to take it for granted.

Let us imagine communication without body language. When we write, we use commas, full stops, exclamation marks and question marks to show where pauses in speech occur and to indicate the tone of voice. **If we write with no punctuation, it is the same as talking without body language**. The whole meaning and emphasis of what we are conveying are lost, as the following example shows.

Just as different punctuation can give the same set of words completely different meanings, so changes in our body language will affect the meaning of the overall message we convey. Our tone of voice, posture and gesture can give our message a completely different meaning from the actual words, often without us realizing it.

Unconscious mimicry

As work on body language progressed, it became clear that people tend to **copy** each other's behaviour and posture without realizing it. Sometimes this is to their advantage, sometimes to their distinct disadvantage.

The power of punctuation

Dear John I want a man who knows what love is all about you are generous kind thoughtful people who are not like you admit to being useless and inferior you have ruined me for other men I yearn for you I have no feelings whatsoever when we're apart I can be forever happy will you let me be yours Gloria

If we now add punctuation, we can make the statement meaningful; however, the meaning all depends on where you pause and where you add emphasis.

Dear John,

I want a man who knows what love is all about. You are generous, kind, thoughtful. People who are not like you admit to being useless and inferior. You have ruined me for other men. I yearn for you. I have no feelings whatsoever when we're apart. I can be forever happy. Will you let me be yours?

Gloria

On the other hand, if the emphasis is different, we have:

Dear John,

I want a man who knows what love is. All about you are generous, kind, thoughtful people, who are not like you. Admit to being useless and inferior. You have ruined me. For other men, I yearn. For you, I have no feelings whatsoever. When we're apart, I can be forever happy. Will you let me be?

Yours, Gloria

Mimicry is, in fact, an indirect way of confirming one's common ground with the person you are assessing or aiming to convince. In a sales situation, being aware of the customer's body language and reflecting it in your own can be positively advantageous, providing that you don't go over the top.

Posture congruence

Further refinement of ideas such as these has helped to identify a whole range of attitudes and feelings associated with posture. Determination, attentiveness, curiosity, puzzlement, aloofness, indifference, rejection and self-satisfaction are just some of the more obvious. Even psychiatrists have recognized that they can use their patients' gestures and body postures to distinguish 'genuine' feelings and 'real' concerns from false ones.

Low profile, high gain

It may seem surprising, but sales staff who deliberately avoid the appearance of being dominant players tend to get the best results.

A successful sales pitch depends on appearing **calm**, giving the customer **space**, using **open, friendly gestures** and maintaining a **low profile**. Those who appear too **defensive, pushy** or **aloof** – particularly on the customer's territory – rarely get a look in.

Research into body language has shown that effective management relies on more than just words. We would probably just send notes to each other otherwise. As most of us know, face-to-face interaction is often the critical factor in concluding a successful business deal, and it is central to creating the right kind of rapport in which key decisions are made.

What body language can tell you

The face-to-face interview is still the best way of judging someone's qualities. This is because observing body language tells you the things that people cannot, will not or do not wish to say in words. You will be able to gauge an individual's experience and qualifications from a CV, but you will sum up his or her potential, honesty, confidence and abilities through face-to-face contact.

Intuition

There are, however, certain traps in interpreting another person's body language. Relying purely on 'intuition' is not enough. You may 'have a feeling about someone' but just can't put your finger on what it is.

In the selection interview, for example, we often hear people say, 'I felt there was something odd about him', or 'I should have trusted my intuition.' The trouble with this is that we can't always be sure whether we have solid grounds for judging someone, or whether our judgements reflect personal prejudices.

You need to be cautious about interpreting non-verbal signals. Think of them as offering **clues** to someone's character. After all, posture, gesture and intonation are subtle and do not constitute *evidence* or *proof* of how a person thinks or feels. In any case, it is rarely one gesture or posture but more often a **combination** of body signals that convey the clues. It is also important to put the signals **in context**: for instance, people may fold their arms because they are more comfortable like that, not because they are being defensive. The point here is that you need to consider the **relevance of the action** to the situation in hand.

Seeing is believing

Giving presentations certainly benefits from visual aids, but a presentation can flop if the presenter fails to connect with the audience. This often happens when the person concerned forgets that they are actually the most important visual aid on the stage.

Good presenters need only two things apart from an audience: to be **seen** and to be **heard**. The more assured the performance, the more rounded the impression given. You often hear people saying that they are scared of standing up in front of their colleagues and having to talk. But what they don't realize is that their audience **wants them to succeed**. You are at your least convincing if you treat them like the enemy.

Try a little reverse psychology: instead of fearing their disapproval, enjoy the attention they are giving you. This will enable you to:

● believe in yourself
● establish a rapport with the audience
● communicate your motives and aims effectively.

The most important visual aid is you

Body words

Sometimes, the expressions that people use – the words they actually speak – offer an indication of the link between body language and *states of mind*.

For example, when someone is relaxed and comfortable with themselves, we say they are 'laid back', and when they are depressed they appear 'down in the mouth'. You get 'jumpy' when you are nervous and 'spit venom' when you are really angry. You have a 'glint in your eye' when something's going well, and you metaphorically 'pin someone down' or 'put them on the spot' when you aim to get answers. We use 'body words' like this in our speech all the time without even realizing it.

Despite the regularity with which we use such expressions, we are rarely *aware* of the connections between what's on our mind and how we behave. By becoming more aware of them we can use such knowledge to our advantage.

For a glossary of body language terms, see the end of the book. Why not test yourself by thinking of terms that you feel reflect states of mind?

The voice

The volume, tone, pitch, speed and fluency of our voice are also part of body language. We vary the way we use our voice in several ways.

● To add emphasis
This is when we increase the volume and rate of speech, or place stress on certain words and phrases.

● To convey emotion
Sadness is characterized by low volume, solemn tone, a deeper voice quality than normal, slower speech and uniform stress upon the words. *Happiness* is characterized by higher volume, sharper tones, stress on key words and phrases, faster speech and a more breathless voice quality.

To provide punctuation
We do this by means of head nods, gestures, changes of pitch and breaking eye contact.

To indicate nervousness or deception
We do this through speech errors such as mispronunciations, unfinished sentences, coughs, omissions, stuttering or stammering (where these are not our normal way of speaking).

Look into my eyes

Eye contact is a fundamental part of getting on with people and gaining their trust. It regulates the flow of communication. When it is lacking, it's easy for misunderstandings to take place. There's nothing worse than making an effort to communicate when those you're addressing can't be bothered to look at you or stare at the wall behind your head.

We make eye contact when we are:

- showing interest
- displaying recognition
- inviting attention
- reinforcing speech
- revealing preferences.

The **casual glance** indicates awareness without sustained interest, whereas the **gaze** conveys genuine interest or intent. Unlike both of these, the **stare** can be intrusive and result in eye contact being broken off. **Holding a look** for a few seconds indicates our awareness of what is being said and a readiness to communicate further.

Waiters in restaurants often use a technique of avoiding eye contact with their customers until it suits them to look at you, thereby giving the clear message: 'I'm too busy to deal with you at the moment.' When they finally do look at you directly, you know that you are about to be attended to.

Studies have found that we maintain eye contact with people 40 per cent of the time when we are talking to them but for 75 per cent of the time when they are talking to us. As listeners, it is important for us to show that we are being attentive to what is being said. Another reason for maintaining eye contact is to determine the sincerity of the speaker. We sum up how we feel about them by observing the clues they offer about themselves.

'Too busy to deal with you...'

One of the first things that managers are told when giving presentations is to **maintain eye contact with the audience** and not to let their eyes wander. Communicators who stick to this simple rule are likely to be seen as more persuasive, truthful, sincere, credible, skilled, informed, experienced, honest and friendly.

The mark of the confident presenter is to maintain eye contact in a *random* fashion, thereby keeping the audience on its toes. Beware the pitfalls of looking at those you like, or focusing on a friendly face, as this tends to distract you, with the result that you lose the attention of your audience.

However unjust it may seem, the confident manager with little knowledge can often outperform the shy but well-informed manager who fails to observe the eye contact rule.

The mind's eye

The body of research called **neuro-linguistic programming** has suggested that we 'think' in terms of *pictures, sounds* and *feelings* and, to a lesser extent, *smells* and *tastes* and that the 'mind's eye' interprets the information we draw from the world around us in terms of these senses:

- visual – thinking in pictures
- auditory – thinking in sounds
- kinaesthetic – thinking in feelings
- olfactory – thinking in terms of smell
- gustatory – thinking in terms of taste.

For example, **visual thinkers** often use phrases such as 'I see that', 'it seems clear to me', 'we should focus on' and 'this throws light upon,' whereas **auditory thinkers** tend to use phrases like 'that sounds good to me' and 'that strikes a chord with me'. **Kinaesthetic thinkers** often use emotive language like 'I warm to that', 'it feels good to me' and 'it's having quite an impact'.

In the West, roughly half of us think in terms of feelings, four in ten in pictures and two in ten in sounds, whereas in the East it is more common for people to think in terms of smell and taste as well. For Westerners, smell and taste act as 'triggers' to the primary senses of seeing, hearing and feeling, such as when the smell of garlic being cooked evokes feelings experienced during a memorable Mediterranean holiday.

We are necessarily *aware* of what we are observing. Our 'data banks' store the knowledge from our senses and call on them subconsciously when it is required. But our body language reflects how the mind's eye is working, revealing how we feel, how we react and how we perform.

What is interesting about these **systems of thinking** is that they influence both the **choice of words** we use and the **body language** we exhibit. Eyes are especially good at indicating what we are thinking. The direction in which they move tells us whether someone is picturing, hearing or feeling. For example:

- looking upwards to left or right indicates that you are thinking visually

- looking sideways to left or right suggests that you are listening, or thinking in sounds
- looking right and down indicates that you are examining your feelings.

We also tend to:

- look up and to the left when we remember images from the past
- look up and to the right when constructing a mental picture from words
- look to the left when we remember sounds
- look to the right when constructing sounds
- look to the left and down when talking to ourselves
- stare straight ahead when visualizing.

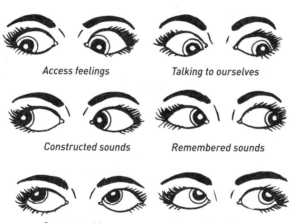

Access feelings   *Talking to ourselves*

Constructed sounds   *Remembered sounds*

Constructed images   *Remembered images*

Visualizing

Body thinking

The point about all this is that, if thinking processes are reflected in the way we use our eyes, they probably manifest themselves in other forms of body language as well. In their book *Introducing Neuro-Linguistic Programming* (2003), Joseph O'Connor and John Seymour wrote, 'As the body and mind are inseparable, how we think always shows somewhere, if you know where to look. In particular, it shows in **breathing patterns, skin colour and posture**.'

What evidence is there to back up such a claim? The same authors give the following examples.

Thinking in visual images

When people do this, they tend to speak more quickly and at a higher pitch. In addition, their breathing may be higher in the chest and shallower. There is often an increase in muscle tension, particularly in the shoulders, the head will be up and the face will often appear paler than normal.

Thinking in sounds

In this case, people tend to breathe evenly over the whole chest area. Small rhythmic movements of the body are discernible and voice tonality is clear, expressive and resonant. The head is well balanced on the shoulders, or held slightly at an angle, as if listening to something.

Talking to oneself

When people do this, they often lean their heads to one side, nestling it on their hand or fist. This is known as the 'telephone position', as one gets the impression that they are talking on an invisible telephone. They may actually repeat out loud what they have just 'heard', with the result that you can see their lips move.

Thinking about feelings

This is characterized by deep breathing low in the stomach area. The voice has a deeper tonality to it and the individual will typically speak slowly, using long pauses. Rodin's famous sculpture of *The Thinker* suggests kinaesthetic thinking.

SUNDAY

MONDAY

TUESDAY

WEDNESDAY

THURSDAY

FRIDAY

SATURDAY

Using gestures

It has also been observed that, when we are involved in different kinds of thinking processes, we often gesture towards the sense organ related to it. For example, some people gesture in the direction of their ears while 'listening' to sound cues; others point to their eyes when 'visualizing'. If we 'feel' things particularly strongly, we sometimes gesture towards the abdomen.

These examples indicate how people think in relation to how they act, but they don't tell us *what* they are thinking. Nevertheless, if you are a coach, counsellor or selection interviewer who needs to be able to interpret sensory clues, you will find these techniques useful.

Getting it together

What does all this tell the manager about the relationship between body language and thought processes? It tells us that, if we are talking with other people during coaching, training, sales, counselling or other similar situations and we are thinking in different 'modes', the chances are that we aren't going to relate to one another easily.

What can occur is that a conversation between a person thinking **visually** and a person thinking in **feelings** turns out to be a frustrating experience for both parties. The visual thinker will probably be tapping a foot impatiently because the 'feeling' thinker 'can't see' the point.

With the advantage of knowing that we think in different modes, we can perhaps fine-tune our response by bringing our use of words into line with the person we are talking to.

- **Visual thinkers** are more likely to use 'visual expressions' such as 'I *see* what you mean', 'Let's get this in *focus*' or 'It seems *hazy* to me.'
- **Auditory thinkers** would be likely to say such things as 'That *sounds* odd to me' or 'I *hear* what you say.'

17

- **Kinaesthetic thinkers** would say such things as 'It doesn't *feel* right to me', 'My *gut* reaction is to say no', or 'I can't *grasp* that idea.'

Establishing rapport

If you want to establish a rapport with someone, being 'on the same wavelength' is a good start. For example, by reflecting similar speech patterns, the sensitive manager indicates that he or she is *on the same wavelength* and will maintain rapport with greater confidence. Managers noted for their social skills often subconsciously adopt similar speech patterns and words.

So, if you find yourself feeding back a few of the words that the other person is using because you feel you are on common ground, it is probably due to your increasing awareness of them. You are becoming more **socially and emotionally 'tuned in'**.

Always judge body language in the context of the situation and look for clusters of signals to reinforce your interpretation.

SUNDAY

MONDAY

TUESDAY

WEDNESDAY

THURSDAY

FRIDAY

SATURDAY

Summary

Today we learned that actions often speak louder than words: less than 10 per cent of what we communicate face to face is in the form of words. Body language tells you things that people cannot, will not or do not wish to say. Talking without body language is the same as writing without punctuation, and learning to interpret body language can enhance our understanding of what someone wishes to convey.

We learned that we should judge body language in the context of a situation and be aware of how our own body language affects others. For example, a successful sales pitch depends on appearing calm, giving the customer space, using open, friendly gestures and maintaining a low profile.

Neuro-linguistic programming (NLP) suggests that we 'think' in terms of pictures, sounds, feelings, smells and tastes, and that being 'on the same wavelength' enables us to establish rapport. Body language expressions such as *laid back* indicate states of mind and can add emphasis, convey emotion, provide 'punctuation' or indicate nervousness. Managers noted for their social skills often unconsciously 'mimic' others' body language and adopt similar patterns of speech.

Tomorrow we will look at the body language of posture and gesture.

Fact-check [answers at the back]

1. What percentage of the meaning we communicate face to face is in the form of words?
   a) 20 per cent ❏
   b) 10 per cent ❏
   c) 40 per cent ❏
   d) 90 per cent ❏

2. What does 'body language' refer to?
   a) Body posture, facial expressions and gestures ❏
   b) All non-verbal communication ❏
   c) Managing without words ❏
   d) Silent clues ❏

3. Talking without body language is the same as what?
   a) Giving a clear message ❏
   b) Being unemotional ❏
   c) Writing without punctuation ❏
   d) Presenting without visual aids ❏

4. What does 'posture congruence' mean?
   a) Adopting a similar posture to the person you are talking to ❏
   b) Adopting a contrary posture ❏
   c) Mimicking the other person's speech and gestures ❏
   d) Calling attention to yourself ❏

5. Why do psychiatrists observe their clients' body language?
   a) To see what they are suffering from ❏
   b) To see if they are hiding behind expressive gestures ❏
   c) As a means of understanding depression ❏
   d) As a way of assessing true feelings and concerns ❏

6. Why is the face-to-face interview valuable?
   a) For seeing what people look like ❏
   b) For offering clues as to a person's motives and feelings ❏
   c) So that the person can tell us about their experience ❏
   d) So that we can see the person's certificates and qualifications ❏

7. What percentage of the time do we observe body language when listening?
   a) 40 per cent ❏
   b) 90 per cent ❏
   c) 75 per cent ❏
   d) The same amount of time whether talking or listening ❏

8. In NLP, what are visual thinkers' eyes said to do?
   a) Move up and to the left or right ❏
   b) Move horizontally to left or right ❏
   c) Move down to the left ❏
   d) Stare straight ahead ❏

9. What are people who 'think in feelings' known as?
a) Visual thinkers ☐
b) Auditory thinkers ☐
c) Kinaesthetic thinkers ☐
d) Gustatory thinkers ☐

10. What can sitting with your arms folded suggest?
a) Superiority ☐
b) Shyness ☐
c) Defensiveness ☐
d) Boredom ☐

MONDAY

Actions speak louder

If you think you can hide behind words, think again. More than likely, your posture and gestures will give you away. As listeners, we subconsciously assess other people's body talk before making up our minds about them, and others do the same to us.

You can often tell someone's attitude from their body language. It's as if they physically 'dance to the tune of their thoughts', conveying *meaning* and *feeling* through their actions. Their head movements, gesticulations and body positions emphasize what they are saying, adding to the impression they create.

While body posture *subconsciously* reflects personality, mood, temperament and intention, gestures are movements that *consciously* convey emotion and meaning. When you 'make a gesture towards somebody', you could just as easily be raising a hand in agreement as raising your fist to them. You may not know *exactly* what you are doing, but you will soon be aware of the impression you are giving.

Today we will look at how the way we 'come across' to others has a lot to do with the body language we exhibit. The more you are aware of it, the more successful your dealings with others will be.

Posture and gesture

Trying to hide behind the words you use without giving yourself away is a waste of time unless you are a particularly good actor. This is because your movements, actions and gestures will soon reveal more about you than you say.

Many types of posture and a variety of gestures – like **raising your eyebrows** when you meet someone – are common to people of all cultures, while others, especially certain **hand gestures**, are culturally specific and you have to be careful how you use them in different countries.

For example, when the thumb and forefinger make a circle, this means 'OK' in the USA, while in Brazil it represents an insult similar to the British 'V' sign and the American raised middle finger. In Japan, however, it means 'money' and in France 'zero'.

UK & USA: OK   *Japan: money*

Brazil: insult   *France: zero*

In Europe, scratching your head can mean you are puzzled about something, whereas in Japan it is often an indication of anger.

SUNDAY

MONDAY

TUESDAY

WEDNESDAY

THURSDAY

FRIDAY

SATURDAY

Communicating actively

We not only make assumptions about people's moods and feelings from postures and gestures, but also tend to view those who exhibit a greater variety of body language in a more positive light. Studies have shown that people who communicate non-verbally through **active movement** tend to be rated as **warm**, more **casual**, **agreeable** and **energetic**, while those who **remain still** are seen as **logical**, **cold** and **analytical**.

Posture

You can often tell a person's attitude from their body posture. How a person **stands** can indicate not only how they feel, but also how they 'view' a situation – in other words, their **attitude towards** someone or something. For example:

- **anger** tends to be conveyed by leaning forward, sometimes with fists clenched and a 'tight' facial expression
- **excitement** is often exhibited in an open body position, arms raised, palms open, with mouth and eyes wide open
- **shyness** is usually conveyed by looking down, making little eye contact and leaning to one side
- **rejection** tends to be exhibited by turning the face and body away.

Intimidation

A very upright (uptight?) stance can appear threatening, particularly when someone invades your territory (such as your office) by marching in and standing close to you. Senior managers who act in this way towards their subordinates are, not surprisingly, viewed as **intimidating**. To maintain rapport with others it is advisable, particularly if you are tall, to reduce your height. Lean on something or stoop slightly.

People of high status often stand **arms akimbo** – hands on hips with elbows turned out. This is a posture of **superiority** and exemplifies **dominance**.

Depressed

Rejecting

Excited

Defensive

Thoughtful

Confident

Superiority posture

Sitting with legs in the four-cross position (with the ankle of one leg resting on the knee of the other) with elbows outstretched and hands clasped behind the neck, head or back similarly suggests someone who wants to convey superiority. It is not uncommon to see two equal-status male managers in discussion subconsciously adopting similar postures in order to maintain their respective positions of authority.

Defensiveness

When you see someone in a meeting sitting with arms crossed, what do you make of it? True, this often happens when chairs have no armrests, but it could mean that the person concerned is being **defensive**. Hunching of the back or clenching of the fists – even if the individual is unaware that this is happening – can be interpreted as **aggressive-defensive**, or even **hostile**.

Defensive posture

Interest and indifference

Posture reflects not only feelings but also **intentions**. These are quite commonly observed in meetings between buyers or senior executives when they are evaluating each other's comments.

Leaning forward in your chair suggests that you are **reacting positively** to what you are hearing and that you may be about to act upon a particular suggestion. On the other

SUNDAY
MONDAY
TUESDAY
WEDNESDAY
THURSDAY
FRIDAY
SATURDAY

hand, leaning back tends to indicate **indifference** or a lack of interest.

Seated readiness posture

People subconsciously indicate **positive interest** in others by propping their heads up on a hand with the index finger pointing up over the cheek. **Critical appraisal** is similarly indicated by an attentive gaze with the chin resting on a thumb and the fingers touching or covering the mouth.

Inappropriate posture

Inappropriate body language can be insulting or annoying. Coming across as too forceful, or too relaxed, can be offensive to others. For example, sitting slumped in a chair with your head down when someone is talking to you displays indifference towards the speaker. Similarly, sitting with one leg over the arm of a chair suggests casual indifference.

As a rule of thumb, avoid over-casual body language, particularly in situations where you are dealing with valued clients or subordinates. It will diminish your own status.

Cultural differences can sometimes lead to erroneous conclusions about posture. American men, for example, often sit with their legs in a four-cross pattern. European men will often just cross one leg over the other, which some in the USA perceive as effeminate.

Male body language in the company of women during meetings sometimes produces the unexpected. One study found that, when a woman was present in a standing group, men who were attracted to her pointed their feet in her direction – even while they were talking to their male colleagues.

Copycat behaviour

We have already referred to posture congruence, in which people imitate or mirror each other's posture without realizing it. **Interactional synchronizing occurs when people simultaneously move at the same time in the same way**, such as when picking up coffee cups or starting to speak at exactly the same moment. This often occurs when we are getting on well together. It is almost as if we are 'echoing' one another. In fact, we are responding subliminally to our partners' subtle cues.

Male pair and female pair exhibiting posture congruence

Opening up

It takes time for people to feel comfortable with a superior. As many body language experts will testify, if you can get an individual to open up physically, the chances are that he or she will open up emotionally as well. Crossed arms, legs or ankles, self-hugging, chin down and a slumped appearance are all telltale signs that something is wrong.

Writing on the subject of bullying at work, the relationship specialist Julie Hay (1996) points out that: 'When you are bullied, you may feel depressed and this makes you slump down and lean forward. If you try standing up straight instead, you can't feel depressed properly!' Conversely, she adds that we tense up, clench our fists and tighten the jaw when we are angry, so that being persuaded to 'lighten up' can have the effect that 'you can't feel angry properly'.

What this means is that, as a manager, you need to find a way to break the ice gently. One way to do this is to offer tea or coffee. Though this may sound simplistic, it is nevertheless the case that people find it difficult to raise a cup to their mouths with their legs crossed, and impossible with their arms crossed. By such a simple procedure, you enable your 'closed' individual literally to 'open up'.

Gesture

If body posture subconsciously reflects attitude, mood and intention, gestures involve a greater degree of *conscious awareness* of how feelings influence actions. We generally gesture with our hands, arms, head and shoulders in order **to add emphasis** to what we are saying.

Head and shoulder gestures

Active interest, listening and concern

A common gesture of television interviewers and their guests is the head cock, where the head is tilted to one side. This indicates **active listening**, interest and concern. Nodding the head slowly while listening indicates 'I hear what you say', whereas more rapid nods mean 'I agree with you.'

A word of warning to interviewers – the head nod that one generally regards as meaning 'yes' means 'no' in Bulgaria, parts of Greece, Turkey, Iran and Bengal!

Confidence, aloofness, submission, aggression

Holding the head up with the face pointing upwards usually indicates **confidence**, but it may also indicate **aloofness** or even **dominance**. Lowering the head and avoiding eye contact is more suggestive of **submissive** behaviour. Thrusting the head and chin forward signals **alarm** or **aggression**, particularly if the eyes are wide open.

Don't care, waste of time

A common gesture is the **shrug**, where both shoulders are raised and hands are held palms up. This usually indicates that the person **doesn't care**, **doesn't know**, or thinks whatever is happening is **a waste of time**.

Disagreement

Certain gestures can appear at variance with what we are saying. Take the case where you say yes but move your head slightly from side to side. You may be buying time or not wanting to appear to disagree, but you are actually signalling *dis*agreement. Your *real* feelings are indicated by the **head shake**.

'**Picking lint**' – picking imaginary pieces of fluff off your clothes – can also signal disagreement. Consciously or not, you are saying 'I don't agree with you, but I can't be bothered to argue about it.'

Hand and arm gestures

The handshake – strength or weakness?

Between countries and cultures similar gestures have different meanings and can easily give rise to misunderstandings. For example, one of the most commonly used gestures in organizational life is the handshake.

- In the USA and western Europe a **firm handshake** is associated with positiveness, conviction, strength, openness and honesty.
- In the Indian subcontinent a **limp handshake** is the norm, representing a different perception of what is positive.

31

Hand cupping – domination and control

Hand gestures can be used to express negative as well as positive feelings, such as annoyance, aggression and insult. People who choose to shake hands by placing one hand over the other person's hand – **cupping** – are demonstrating their confidence, authority or even dominance.

Fist and finger insults

Fist waving, the 'V' sign and the single finger pointing upwards are all insults. In fact, pointing – known as **battoning** – is generally regarded as rude or aggressive and should be avoided wherever possible in business interaction. It is more socially acceptable to direct an upraised palm than to point towards someone when in a meeting.

Though in much of Europe tapping the forefinger on the side of the head is widely recognized as signifying 'you're crazy', the Dutch tap the centre of the forehead, while the French 'screw' the finger into the side of the head.

The hand shrug – mock honesty

In conversation, a palms-up gesture tends to indicate **uncertainty**, though with a degree of **honesty.** But it can also be used to deceive. The **hand shrug**, as it is known, is one of those **mock honesty** gestures that appear to enlist our sympathy by giving the impression that the other person has our best interests at heart.

Mock honesty: 'Trust me – I'm in marketing!'

Patting, tapping, thumping, fiddling

If you raise your eyebrows while placing your hands palms down in a 'patting' fashion, you indicate **satisfaction** with, or **certainty** about, something. If this 'patting' continues, it can mean 'I have heard what you have to say so please calm down.' Tapping one's fingers on a desk is a clear sign of impatience, while banging or thumping indicates **annoyance** and **aggression**. Fiddling with pencils during meetings suggests **boredom** or **irritation**.

Steepling – confidence, certainty

A gesture commonly seen in organizational life is **steepling**, where both hands are close together with fingertips touching and the palms a short distance apart – making the shape of a church steeple. Often unconsciously performed, this action indicates **confidence**, **thoughtfulness** or having reached a **decision**. You often see this in sales situations.

Steepling

Palm rocking – 'maybe'

Another hand gesture often noticed among managers is **palm rocking** with fingers spread out. Amusingly termed the 'so-so', it involves the palm being face down and rocked from side to side. It is equivalent to the verbal '-ish', meaning 'maybe', 'possibly', 'ok-ish'.

Thumbs up

You would think that the ubiquitous 'thumbs up' gesture would be commonly understood as meaning 'OK' or 'everything's fine'. But it isn't.

- In Australia, if made with a jerk, it means 'Up yours!'
- In Nigeria, parts of Italy and Greece it is regarded as an insult.
- In Germany, when you order drinks, it means 'One please.'

Deception gestures

We often gesture without being aware of it, and being able to read these gestures in others can be revealing.

The nose touch or tap

People often touch their nose when they are not telling the truth or when they believe someone is trying to deceive them. A tap on the side of the nose with a forefinger differs in meaning between cultures:

- In Britain and Sardinia, it conveys complicity, confidentiality or secrecy.
- In Italy it means 'Be alert!'

A tap on the end of the nose means 'Mind your own business!' in Britain, Holland and Austria.

Scratching

Scratching one's neck below the ear with the index finger a few times, with the neck turned slightly to one side, indicates doubt and uncertainty. You often see this among car mechanics who also tend to suck in air between the teeth when asked how long it will take, and how much it will cost, to repair your car...

'Keep it a secret!'

Rubbing one's eye

When they are not telling the truth, people sometimes rub their eye while looking down, as if they are distracted by a piece of grit. This gesture is designed to distract the attention of the listener.

Placing a hand over the nose

This gesture can in some situations suggest both fear and disbelief – as if you don't want to accept what is happening.

SUNDAY
MONDAY
TUESDAY
WEDNESDAY
THURSDAY
FRIDAY
SATURDAY

Summary

Today you learned more about what body language can reveal. People physically 'dance to the tune of their thoughts'. You learned that body posture *subconsciously* reflects personality, mood and intention, while gestures *consciously* convey emotion and meaning.

People who communicate non-verbally through active movement tend to be rated warm, casual, agreeable and energetic, whereas people who are still are often seen as cold and analytical. When people are getting on well, they often move at the same time, in the same way.

You can improve your communication skills when you understand the meaning of different postures and gestures, taking into account cultural differences. For example, it's useful to know that an upright posture may be intended to intimidate, and that hands on hips, crossed legs, and hands behind the head aim to convey superiority, while folded arms suggest defensiveness.

Likewise, you will sense a positive attitude from someone sitting leaning forward or propping their head on their hand with an index finger pointing up their cheek. You have also learned about the gestures people use when they are trying to deceive you. The more aware you are of body language, the better you will be at dealing with others.

Fact-check [answers at the back]

1. What does standing upright with hands on hips indicate?
   a) Boredom ☐
   b) Dominance ☐
   c) Confusion ☐
   d) Submission ☐

2. What do folded arms, crossed legs, chin down, imply?
   a) Feeling comfortable ☐
   b) Being about to open up ☐
   c) Feeling uncomfortable ☐
   d) Feeling confident ☐

3. What do moving simultaneously and using similar gestures suggest?
   a) They have established rapport ☐
   b) They disagree ☐
   c) They want to impress the other person ☐
   d) They feel uncomfortable in the other person's company ☐

4. What does head up, face pointing upwards, indicate?
   a) Submission ☐
   b) Aggression ☐
   c) Shyness ☐
   d) Confident aloofness ☐

5. What does the shoulder shrug indicate?
   a) A caring attitude ☐
   b) Not caring, not knowing ☐
   c) Submissiveness ☐
   d) Having all the answers ☐

6. What does picking lint (fluff) off one's clothes suggest?
   a) The person feels untidy ☐
   b) The person is in agreement ☐
   c) The person is bored ☐
   d) The person can't be bothered to argue ☐

7. What does palms open and turned up mean?
   a) Confidence and agreement ☐
   b) Certainty and confidence ☐
   c) Shyness and avoidance ☐
   d) Honesty and/or uncertainty ☐

8. What does 'steepling' the fingers indicate?
   a) Reaching or having reached a decision ☐
   b) Waiting for someone's response ☐
   c) Disagreement ☐
   d) Lack of confidence ☐

9. What does rubbing an eye and looking down suggest?
   a) Boredom ☐
   b) Interest ☐
   c) Shyness ☐
   d) Deception ☐

10. What does palms down and in a rocking motion indicate?
    a) Having come to a decision ☐
    b) Certainty ☐
    c) Maybe, possibly ☐
    d) Honesty ☐

TUESDAY

Power and influence

Successful management of people depends on positive leadership. Without it you have little more than the exercise of power. People get where they are because they adopt various strategies for increasing their authority over others. Managers who are coercive, aggressive or manipulative will find that these uses of power can be self-defeating, destroying motivation and loyalty. People who are too submissive often lose out in the promotion stakes, while those who maintain the right balance between assertiveness and self-assurance climb the ladder.

Success has as much to do with *being seen* to do your job well as actually doing it well. It's a simple (although perhaps not always welcome) fact of life that conveying the right impression can make up for deficiencies in knowledge and skills. Many talented people fail to gain promotion because they make the mistake of thinking that success is judged on the basis of *what* they do well, rather than the *impression* they create in doing it.

Understanding body language can enable managers to become more effective, but **leadership skills** involve more than this. Simply being aware of how people function isn't the same as demonstrating your willingness to listen or to connect with their needs.

The body language of power

When you hear people being described as 'aggressive', 'manipulative', 'assertive' or 'submissive', what kind of mental picture do you have of them? Many of the words we use to describe how colleagues present themselves at work have direct parallels in body language.

The body language of power

	Description	Body language
Aggressive	Angry, sarcastic, being a bad listener, putting people down, blaming others, shouting, speaking in a raised voice, being critical	Clenched fists, tense body posture, hands on hips, confrontational pose, finger pointing, narrowing eyes, looking down on others
Manipulative	Patronizing, crafty, calculating, insincere, two-faced, a 'user', lacking trust, over-friendly, making ends justify means, contrived	Exaggerated gestures (e.g. open palms to indicate 'deliberate' sincerity), overly laid-back postures, 'patronizing' touching, exaggerated eye contact, 'sugary' voice, patting
Submissive	Apologetic, self-deprecating, resentful, low self-esteem, retreating, too ready to please	Fidgety, covering mouth and eyes, imitative, slumped posture, nervous disposition, fiddling, poor eye contact, quiet, faltering voice, 'pleading' smile, obsequiousness
Assertive	Sincere, open, honest, respectful, sympathetic, firm but fair, offering constructive criticism, good listener, offering praise where it is due, treating people as equals	Upright relaxed posture, face-to-face eye contact, calm and open gestures, relaxed facial expression, maintaining reasonable distance from subject, resonant speech, clear hand signals

The good manager

Successful managers are those who feel comfortable about being assertive and display their expertise and leadership qualities through **self-assured, confident behaviour**. The professional manager who is 'firm but fair' generally feels more confident about handling difficult situations, gets the best out of people, improves business outcomes and actually reduces conflict.

People operate in a variety of different ways at work.

- Some individuals are just plain **pushy** and try to 'get round the boss' in order to raise their own status at the expense of colleagues.
- Others try to influence their superiors by being **subservient**. This is when you hear derogatory comments about 'crawling', or being 'a creep' – behavioural characteristics which Dickens epitomized in the character of the obsequious Uriah Heep.
- People who 'lower themselves' physically diminish the respect due to them.

When we describe someone as 'straight', we mean open and honest, while 'bent' signifies the opposite. Similarly, someone who is 'upright' is to be **trusted**, and the person who 'walks tall' feels confident and proud. Individuals who see others as inferior 'look down on' or 'look down their noses at' them. These are body language expressions of **contempt**.

'Keeping someone at arm's length' or 'not crowding their space', means literally not getting **too close** to them. On the other hand, when someone is said to be 'close to the boss', you assume that the boss is *allowing* that person to occupy his or her physical space. Similarly, when we say 'she has the boss's ear', we mean she is close enough to say things in private. 'He's the boss's right-hand man' signifies not only **personal influence** but **close liaison** with someone in authority.

Five sources of power

People get to positions of power by adopting various different strategies for increasing their authority over others. French and Raven (1968) refer to these as **sources of power**:

- *position* – who they are
- *coercive* – how tough they are
- *reward* – how supportive they are
- *expertise* – how informed they are
- *charisma* – how unique they are.

1 Position power

John Title

'My power in this organization comes from people knowing who I am. I'm a Senior Supervisor and this means that staff should respect my authority. We should look up to our superiors; after all, that's what **'super'** – **'above'** – **'visor'** – **'look'** means. Others look up to me. I have access to the boss because of my position in the company.'

People still tend to obey managers out of respect for their title, even if that individual fails in all other aspects of the job. Powerbrokers who rely on **who they are** in an organization are not difficult to spot. They adopt the postures, gestures and unspoken mannerisms associated with hierarchical authority. Even the most casual observer can generally pick out the 'boss' in such a group from the various kinds of body language displayed. Typically, the boss will adopt a 'posture of superiority' to which the subordinates defer.

The significant thing about position power is that it is the minimum form of authority that a manager has. **Status symbols** are all-important, like having one's own office, company car, uniform, carpet and designated place to sit in meetings. The concern here is to **maintain image and reinforce authority**.

Case study: position power

A manager we came across used to make people wait outside his door for longer than might be expected after they had knocked, and then shout, 'Come in!' in an irritated tone. This had the effect of making the employee feel uncomfortable about entering the manager's **territory**. The manager would continue writing, giving the impression that he was not to be disturbed. After a further period he would look up while replacing his pen-top and, with a degree of impatience, tell the unfortunate individual to go back and close the door. Through *intimidatory* body language and *tone* of voice he was reminding his **subordinate** of their **relative positions**.

In recent years, cyclical changes in general economic conditions have brought about a fundamental reappraisal of organizational structures and patterns of employment, with the result that attitudes to hierarchical authority have altered. **Horizontal** (expertise-driven) rather than **vertical** (position-driven) lines of authority make for greater co-operation and encourage upskilling.

The acceptance of more egalitarian approaches to employment and management has been shown to increase personal commitment to employers and to boost production.

At the Mars company in Slough, England, for example, employees wear similar uniforms, to emphasize greater equality and lessen the distinction between superiors and subordinates. Many large organizations today are dispensing with the term 'manager' altogether, preferring instead designations such as coach, team member and team leader to reinforce team spirit. Managers are expected to **facilitate**, not merely **administrate**. It may well be that the term 'manager' will disappear in the same way that foreman, charge-hand and supervisor are slowly going. With their disappearance we are witnessing the **decay of position power** and the **rise of reward and expert power.**

2 Coercive power

Phil Hardman

'You have to be tough and decisive to manage. If managers fail to take on or discipline idle employees, the rest of the workforce won't respect them. Threats enhance respect for a manager. How many times have you heard someone say, "He's fair, but I wouldn't get *on the wrong side* of him if I were you"? The strong manager doesn't "um and err" about things, or ask if everything's OK with you. Just hold your gaze; **stand straight and don't move around** – because it suggests you are wavering.'

The body language of coercion is not difficult to recognize. Its most common expression is **aggression**, which is characterized by postures and gestures designed to threaten or intimidate:

- an upright stance, hands on hips, elbows out
- sitting in a dominant position
- an expressionless or angry gaze
- the invasion of another person's space
- shouting
- finger pointing (batoning)
- staring at a subordinate
- 'strutting' – implying 'don't get in my way'
- turning away when someone else is talking
- snorts of derision, annoyance or disgust
- frowning or jutting the chin out
- clenching the fist
- holding one's lapels with upturned thumbs
- hands in pockets with thumbs sticking out
- looking down the nose at someone.

Coercive power can be self-defeating, however. Threats (negative appraisal, demotion) and non-verbal intimidation (as above) often result in high staff turnover and a demotivated workforce.

To resort to coercive methods when the situation genuinely requires it – firing someone for gross misconduct, for example – may be acceptable, although you need to be clear about your motives.

Never use coercion as a means of boosting your own ego. A **latent threat** of coercive action can prove far more effective.

Finger pointing, or batoning

3 Reward power

Jill Merit

'Staff in my company obey their superiors because they know that they will ultimately be **rewarded** in some way. The culture promotes this. Perhaps we're different, but we know how to keep our employees happy. It's not bribery; it's **sympathetic management**. We are not in a position to increase salaries at the drop of a hat, but we can reward people with more interesting work, a glowing appraisal and more responsibility, giving them a sense of achievement and empowering them.'

Unlike monetary rewards, personal encouragement is conveyed non-verbally through tone of voice and gestures and has to be sincere if you aim to motivate or boost morale. There are many ways in which managers can reward employees in this way, including:

- a longer than average handshake or handclasp to emphasize a job well done
- a light touch or pat on the back to express praise or congratulation – touching someone on the shoulder as they leave is a subtle way of rewarding good rapport
- a smile and a slightly longer gaze to denote thanks
- a slight nod of the head to suggest agreement or recognition.

This might all sound like common sense, but we often use body language expressions in our speech without realizing the connection between the reward and the action. Here are some examples.

- 'I was genuinely touched.'
- 'I have to hand it to you.'
- 'It's only a small gesture.'
- 'You deserve a pat on the back for that.'
- 'Thanks for shouldering the burden.'

4 Expert power

Dr Graham Sure

'Being recognized **experts** in our field increases our **influence** and **control**. How else do you think we get our research funding? This is where the advantages of body language come in. If I appear hesitant, look puzzled, fail to make adequate eye contact, speak without self-assurance, or come across as non-assertive and lacking in confidence, this makes people question my competence, because **I appear** unsure.'

Assertive body language conveys **confidence** and suggests **expertise**. The way you stand or the manner in which you pay attention to others gives an impression of certainty, self-assurance and a sense that you 'feel good about yourself'. Simple things like fixing your gaze on the other person and 'steepling' – where the fingertips are touching but the palms are apart – indicate that you are interested in what you are being told. This kind of relaxed body language exudes confidence. Turning the hands palms down and appearing to press downwards while talking to others also has the effect of making others listen and look up to you.

Research in neuro-linguistic programming has shown that our thought processes condition our potential to succeed or fail. By positive '**self-conditioning**' – maintaining an internal dialogue that reinforces personal successes – we can make ourselves **feel more confident**, which makes us more influential.

The authority of the expert is largely a matter of personal self-confidence, which is reflected in speech. The emphasis placed on certain words is all-important, as shown in the table below.

Expertise and self-confidence

Non-expert	Expert
I **hope** that you will enjoy this presentation.	I **know** you will appreciate what I have to say.
I **think** that is most **probably** the answer.	In these circumstances **this** is what **we should do**.

It's hard to use confident words when you don't display confident posture and gestures, so here are a few tips to help you.

- Use positive-sounding words that emphasize certainty at all times.
- When talking, hold your palms down to express certainty.
- When sitting, try holding your palms apart with fingertips touching to show you are 'in touch'.
- Stand upright, maintain an 'open' stance and smile.
- Walk with an upright posture, as if you know where you are going.
- Hold your head up, but don't look down your nose.
- Tell yourself you are going to succeed.
- Have faith in yourself and your abilities.

5 Charisma power

A fan

'When he walked into the room, I was mesmerized. I couldn't take my eyes off him. I don't know what it was. He had a sort of aura, self-assurance without arrogance – a *presence*. He didn't even have to speak. There were people buzzing around him like flies, and yet he seemed totally unconcerned. I was the one feeling nervous. How lucky to be like that. Some people just have that indefinable quality, don't they, that *je ne sais quoi*?'

Social psychologists have long tried to establish the link between **leadership** and **charisma**. Although we tend to think of it as a unique quality of the individual in the spotlight, it may well be that we help to create the aura in our own minds. In other words, **we invest the person we admire with the power to influence us**. There is undeniably *something* about a charismatic individual, but whether it is sufficient in itself to generate veneration, or the kind of mass hysteria you sometimes witness at music venues, is open to question.

What is clear is that, when a charismatic person enters a room, others tend to move away to give him or her **space**. Sometimes it is simply the hush that descends on the gathering that tells you they are special.

Charismatic people often **seem tall** because observers tend to bow slightly – literally lowering their height – when in their company. They are are also said to **radiate power**, energy, love and so forth.

Sometimes we refer to these special people as being 'head and shoulders above the rest'. These are the ones who are 'up front', 'firm', 'rock steady', even 'having us in the palms of their hands'. We respect them for their leadership, aware that their mere **presence** denotes authority.

Summary

Today we learned that success in management has as much to do with *being seen* to do your job well as actually doing it well. Managers express their authority through posture, gesture and tone of voice rather than through words.

Managers may present themselves at work as aggressive, manipulative, assertive or submissive, and they will show this in their body language. Successful managers feel comfortable about being assertive and display their leadership qualities through confident body language and behaviour.

We learned about the five 'types' of power:

1 position power, the minimum form of authority that a manager has

2 coercive power, which can be self-defeating because it destroys motivation and loyalty

3 reward power, where personal encouragement motivates and boosts morale

4 expert power, where the authority of the expert is suggested by assertive and confident body language

5 charisma power, where we *invest* those we most admire with the power to influence us.

SUNDAY
MONDAY
TUESDAY
WEDNESDAY
THURSDAY
FRIDAY
SATURDAY

Fact-check [answers at the back]

1. Which body posture word/s best describe honesty?
   a) Pushy ❏
   b) Laid back ❏
   c) Bent ❏
   d) Straight ❏

2. How has position power changed in recent years?
   a) It has increased ❏
   b) It has decreased ❏
   c) It has stayed the same ❏
   d) It has become more evident ❏

3. What does coercive body language include?
   a) Steepling the fingers ❏
   b) Finger pointing and strutting ❏
   c) Avoidance of conflict ❏
   d) Holding your palms down when talking ❏

4. What does reward power suggest?
   a) Only offering financial incentives ❏
   b) Rewarding with a smile, nod or touch ❏
   c) Sticking your chin out ❏
   d) Avoiding people's personal space ❏

5. What do managers exercising expert power do?
   a) Lower their height and look down ❏
   b) Stare or look through others ❏
   c) Appear unsure ❏
   d) Use assertive body language ❏

6. How can charismatic power be seen?
   a) In a person's presence or aura ❏
   b) Through the energy a person radiates in public ❏
   c) In the body language of the fans/followers ❏
   d) In the clothes they wear ❏

7. What does assertive body language demonstrate?
   a) Confrontational posture, finger pointing ❏
   b) Open posture, eye contact, clear signals ❏
   c) Exaggerated gestures and eye contact ❏
   d) Fidgety behaviour, slumped posture ❏

8. How do assertive managers behave?
   a) They put people down and blame others ❏
   b) They are devious and insincere ❏
   c) They are apologetic and self-deprecating ❏
   d) They are open, honest and respectful ❏

9. What do successful managers need to do?
   a) Make the company money ❏
   b) Be seen to do well ❏
   c) Keep on the right side of the boss ❏
   d) Be pushy if they want to advance ❏

10. What do effective managers
    need to be?
a) Manipulative ☐
b) Coercive ☐
c) Assertive ☐
d) Aggressive ☐

WEDNESDAY

Performance art

A presentation is essentially a *performance* in which the hearts and minds of your audience must be won over. Since 90 per cent of what we communicate is transmitted non-verbally, a large part of every performance relies upon *presence* rather than words.

Ultimately, there is nothing more visually persuasive than *you yourself*. You can have any amount of technology to support you, but if everyone's looking at the screen rather than at you, you aren't going to come across as convincing. It is perhaps no accident that highly successful presenters are described as having their audiences 'in the palm of their hands': the upturned palm is associated with honesty, openness and sincerity.

Before giving a presentation you need to be clear about what you are trying to achieve. Are you aiming to inform, instruct, justify, persuade or sell? If the objective isn't clear to you, it isn't going to be clear to the audience either. If your body language doesn't match your words you won't be trusted, because what you *say* will be at variance with what you *mean*.

Today you will learn the ten basic rules for giving successful presentations and some tips for encouraging participation. Remember these and you'll soon reap the rewards.

The ten rules of engagement

'Brilliance without the capability
to communicate it is worth little in any
enterprise.'

Thomas Leech, 2004

All good salespeople know that overstating the intention to sell increases the resistance on the part of their clients to buy. The aim of a sales presentation should be to inform and subtly persuade. Whatever the nature of the presentation, subtle use of body language and tone of voice can be as persuasive as words. If you are to be convincing, you need to know the rules.

1 Maintain eye contact with the audience

Members of your audience need to believe that you are talking to them as individuals. They need to feel that your 'random glance' during a sweep of the room is at them in particular and that you are only looking at everyone else out of politeness.

If you maintain regular eye contact with your audience when giving a presentation, you are more likely to be perceived as sincere, credible, honest, experienced, friendly and hence persuasive.

2 Be aware of your hands and voice

If eye contact is important in gaining the attention of your audience, how you **act** and **sound** is just as important in maintaining it. Your hands should conduct your presentation as if it were the slow movement of a symphony, fingers and palms modulating with your words. When presenting facts, it helps to hold the hands out and the palms down as this indicates **assurance** and **certainty**.

'The facts are as follows.'

Conversely, if you hold your palms upwards when delivering facts, you may be perceived as **uncertain** and your message as confusing.

Speak slowly, adding **emphasis** where appropriate by varying the **tone** and **resonance** of your voice. Speaking more quickly to make a particular point is fine, providing that your audience can hear and understand you. Very often, presenters speed up when they start to feel confident about the presentation and 'lose' sections of the audience as a result.

3 Repeat key phrases

One way of adding **emphasis** and reinforcing your message in a presentation is to repeat key phrases using an **assertive tone** of voice. The *actual* words themselves need not always be repeated, providing that the *meaning* remains the same. In selling, for example, one might say, 'There are **four** main selling points to this product. Let us look in detail at **one** and then go through the **other three points**.'

4 Use visual aids for structuring

Maintaining eye contact with the audience while making use of prompting techniques and facilities is not always easy. One method is to use cards, which are held in the palm of the hand and require you to take your eyes off the audience only momentarily. These cards should contain only **keywords** – reminders of what you wish to say – and nothing else.

Another, and perhaps better, way is to use words on the screen or flipchart as **keyword prompts** and as a means of structuring your presentation. This can also be done with the help of a flipchart agenda, enabling you to 'signpost' issues and ideas that indicate your intention to move from one area to the next. Typical expressions that you would use in such situations might be 'moving on now to item three', or 'I would now like to examine the outcome.'

 Whatever you do, don't allow a visual aid to distract you from those you are addressing. The moment you start to pay less attention to the audience, the audience starts to pay less attention to you.

The audience will pay less attention to you if you turn your back

5 Be animated, but stay calm

A number of common distractions can reduce audience attention and make you look less professional. Do not:

- **march** from one side of the stage to the other
- **fiddle** with pointers, pens or other sundry items

- **seek confirmation** with phrases like 'Is that OK?', 'Do you see?' or 'You know what I mean?'
- stand with your **hands in your pockets**; the posture gives the impression that you are over-confident; but, more importantly, if your hands are in your pockets, you cannot use them to gesture and emphasize your words.

6 Sound enthusiastic to hold attention

It is generally accepted that for all presentations there is an **attention curve**. Audience attention will be high at the beginning, low in the middle and higher at the end. If your presentation is long – more than 30 minutes – you should try to hold their attention by sounding more enthusiastic as you go along. Enthusiasm is powerfully expressed through body language and can be infectious.

7 Retain attention by creating a break

Another way of retaining attention is to break in the middle of your presentation to pass round items, samples or papers and literature. However, if you are going to do this, keep the materials hidden from view at the start so that they do not distract attention from you.

8 Take note of negative body language

The more skilled you become in recognizing the meanings implicit in gesture and posture, the more control you will have over your audience. Gestures and postures tell you a lot about people's attitudes towards you and about their **receptiveness** to what you are saying. Here are some examples.

- **Leaning the chin on a hand** with the index finger on the cheek indicates *critical appraisal* or critical evaluation.
- **The steepling gesture** indicates that someone has made up their mind either for or against you.
- **Sitting with arms and ankles crossed** indicates that someone may feel defensive.
- **Picking lint (fluff)** from clothes indicates that someone disagrees but does not want to argue with you.

Critical appraisal

If you are aware of these things happening, try to draw the people concerned into the dialogue. One way of doing this is to invite comments from the audience by directing your line of sight to the individual who seems at odds with what you are saying. For example: 'I'm sure I haven't convinced all of you, so perhaps, you Sir/Madam...what sort of concerns do you feel people might have about this?' By keeping your question impersonal you are more likely to get them to drop their defences and air their views.

Picking lint: silent disagreement

9 Avoid being distracted

Because body language is a two-way process, presenters, whether they are aware of it or not, **respond to cues and signals** given by members of the audience. There are common pitfalls associated with this.

● The presenter may unwittingly direct his or her attention to **the 'friendly' individual** who is clearly paying attention and who nods and occasionally smiles in response to the presenter's points. This breaks the visual link with the rest of the audience.
● **The one-to-one conversation** where the presenter gets caught up in a question-and-answer situation with a single member of the audience all too often makes other members of the audience feel excluded.

10 Encourage convergence of opinions

In any audience there are bound to be differences of opinion. The astute presenter can often identify sets or subgroups of people who appear to share similar opinions. This is particularly important in negotiations or meetings in which the goal is to achieve a consensus.

Encouraging participation

As we have already observed, when people establish a rapport they often mirror each other's gestures and postures (posture congruence). For example, you might be in a meeting in which three people from Personnel and Accounts appear to be sharing the same body posture. The engineers on the other side of the table, however, are sitting stiffly, arms folded. What would you make of this? Would you conclude that the engineers were being defensive and that their body language indicated that much work still needed to be done before they were won over? If so, what would be your strategy for dealing with the situation?

What you need to do is **encourage participation**.

● Mention their names or describe their expertise
Even if you think that you have to flatter or sound a bit ingratiating about people's skills and contributions, it is worth remembering that most people like to be respected and have their views respected too.

● Produce more support for your ideas
You can do this by using the technique previously described as upward appeal. In this case, you would introduce the following kind of statement: 'The Managing Director and I had a long discussion about this very point and he agrees with me...'

Remember that every presentation is essentially a performance, so how you perform is central to the success or failure of what you are trying to communicate.

Summary

Today you've learned that, when giving presentations, there is nothing more visually persuasive than *you yourself*. The best presenters know that subtle use of body language and varying the speed and tone of the voice can have as powerful an effect as the words.

While it's vital to be clear about your objectives in presentations – if *you* aren't, the audience won't be either – you also need to make sure that your performance is effective. Today we have looked at the ten basic rules for giving successful presentations.

1 Maintain eye contact with the audience.
2 Be aware of your hand gestures and tone of voice.
3 Repeat key phrases to reinforce your message.
4 Use visual aids to structure your presentation.
5 Be animated, but stay calm and look professional.
6 Sound enthusiastic to hold the audience's attention.
7 Retain attention by creating a break.
8 Take note of negative body language.
9 Avoid being distracted by members of the audience.
10 Attempt to encourage convergence of opinions.

Every presentation you make is a *performance* that relies upon *presence* as much as words to be successful.

SUNDAY
MONDAY
TUESDAY
WEDNESDAY
THURSDAY
FRIDAY
SATURDAY

Fact-check [answers at the back]

1. What does an effective presenter do?
   a) Uses the screen to capture audience attention ❑
   b) Picks out key listeners and focuses on them ❑
   c) Regularly and randomly scans the audience ❑
   d) Relies on gimmicks to convince ❑

2. What does palms turned down indicate?
   a) Feelings of doubt and uncertainty ❑
   b) A sense of assurance and certainty ❑
   c) You are about to stand up ❑
   d) You cannot be trusted ❑

3. What do 'key messages' need to be?
   a) Stressed once during a presentation ❑
   b) Presented in a passive tone of voice ❑
   c) Repeated and often rephrased ❑
   d) Left on the flipchart to remind people ❑

4. What does having the audience 'in the palm of your hand' mean?
   a) They are bored ❑
   b) They are attentive and want you to continue ❑
   c) They have lost trust in you as presenter ❑
   d) You have lost contact with them ❑

5. What is the best way to maintain audience attention?
   a) March from one side of the stage to the other ❑
   b) Use pointers, board rubbers, etc., for emphasis ❑
   c) Repeat phrases like 'Is that OK?' and 'Do you see?' ❑
   d) Use gestures and posture to reinforce the message ❑

6. What is the key to a successful presentation?
   a) Sound enthusiastic ❑
   b) Keep your body language to a minimum ❑
   c) Let the audio-visual aids do the talking ❑
   d) Wear smart clothes ❑

7. What should you do when looking at the audience?
   a) Fix on those who seem to agree with you ❑
   b) Ignore those who appear to disagree ❑
   c) Exaggerate your expressions to add emphasis ❑
   d) Try to involve those who appear to disagree ❑

8. What is a common fault with presenters?
   a) Maintaining eye contact with the audience ❑
   b) Failing to identify groups with similar interests ❑
   c) Looking for those who disagree ❑
   d) Adding emphasis by posture and gesture ❑

9. If a salesperson makes the 'palms up and open' gesture, what does this suggest?
a) They are absolutely certain ❏
b) They are honest and trustworthy ❏
c) They are being devious ❏
d) They are being blunt and to the point ❏

10. What are the best kind of presentation notes?
a) A script you can stick to ❏
b) Memorized and delivered without prompts ❏
c) PowerPoint headlines or prompt cards ❏
d) Words you can read on the screen ❏

THURSDAY

Selling yourself

There is a well-known but unwritten rule in sales: you need to sell *yourself* before you can successfully sell your product. Selling is the art of persuasion, but it is also the art of *communication.* Since most communication is non-verbal, your body language can make the difference between success and failure.

Deliberately using body language as an aid to selling, however, is to miss the point. You are *not acting* but *negotiating* – harnessing your skills and attributes to gain the trust and commitment of the buyer. The interaction that takes place in sales negotiations is crucial. You ignore it at your peril. This is because buyers have purchasing power, while sellers have to sell in order to justify their positions.

Selling is a *service,* which means there is an expectation that the sales person will respect the buyer's needs. *Push* too hard and you can appear too demanding. *Pull* too early and you risk losing the catch. Appear too ingratiating and you come across as insincere or manipulative. Seem too humble and you appear subservient.

Today you will learn about the five basic ground rules to selling successfully. They all involve body language.

Sales: the ground rules

The five **examples of power** that we discussed on Tuesday – **position**, **coercion**, **reward**, **expertise** and **charisma** – equally apply to you in the sales situation, though with a different emphasis.

Subservience personified

1 Remember who you are

Sellers generally have less power than buyers for the simple reason that buyers can say 'yes', 'no' or 'convince me'.

Over the years, business practice has come to recognize the status differentials between buyers and sellers with the result that more 'significant' titles have been invented to take account of the relative lack of **position power** of sales personnel. Gone are the days when you would wield a small white card saying Sales Representative. Today, you are more likely to carry a title like Regional Sales Director, Brand Manager, Product Consultant or Account Director.

There is always a danger that, if you don't recognize the relative lack of power in your position as a seller, you will irritate, put off or even offend the client. Taking account of this displays your recognition of the other party's need to be respected for showing interest in you and your product. You will need to ensure that you:

- **don't keep the buyer waiting**
- don't allow your **body language** to convey messages of urgency, aggression, arrogance or insincerity
- maintain a **respectable distance** from the client (2–4 ft or 60–120 cm)
- **alter your standing posture** so as not to give the impression of towering over him or her.

Door-to-door sales personnel are instructed to **step back** when someone opens the door. This indicates that they are **non-threatening** and have no intention of invading the client's space. Unfortunately, this rule is often broken.

Having established your position in the transaction, how you speak to the client is all-important. Much of what you **convey** is via the **tone and speed of your voice**, indicating sincerity, trust and reliability.

2 Make the client feel comfortable

Making the client feel comfortable is an essential part of establishing a good rapport. Some sales personnel find that **making notes** during the course of a meeting helps to reinforce the status of the buyer by making him or her **feel** more important. Others bring gifts and free samples with them – think of all the pens and pads that medical reps leave behind in doctors' surgeries.

If you give something to a client, however small, you are effectively 'rewarding' them in advance for agreeing to buy your product. Once they accept, they will often find it more difficult to say no.

The seller needs to make the buyer feel like **a valued customer,** so a small gift may be a subtle way of rewarding his or her continuing interest. However, take care that your gift is not interpreted as a bribe.

The interaction between buyer and seller should be **rewarding to the buyer**, if you want to see him or her again. Selling is a sophisticated business and, without **self-assurance** and a **convincing manner**, no amount of information, gifts or promises will work for you. A relaxed manner and a sense of humour are often all that are needed to win the day.

A relaxed manner will win the day

3 Use subtle persuasion, not coercion

If rewarding the buyer is part of the psychology of successful selling, it stands to reason that coercion is not. You are seeking to **inform and subtly persuade**, not to bully or manipulate. The buyer, of course, may try to manipulate you, which is why you need all your faculties about you.

Buyers can get away with being aggressive towards the seller, being rude when it suits them and winding you up just to see how far you can be pushed. They will often use postures and gestures that reinforce their **purchasing power** and – while you may be seething under the surface – it's your job to stay cool and ensure that you manage the situation. That way you will come out the winner.

By taking note of the buyer's body language, you will soon learn to judge how he or she is responding.

● **Superiority** can be deduced from a posture in which the hands are clasped round the back of the head with the elbows pointing out sideways.

- **Critical evaluation** tends to be indicated by the chin leaning on an upward-pointing index finger.
- **Impatience** is shown by fingers drumming on a hard surface, combined with sideways glances and snorts of disagreement.
- **Disagreement**, or even disbelief, is demonstrated by the head being shaken slightly from side to side.
- **Understanding** is shown by a slow nodding of the head, while nodding more quickly indicates agreement.
- **Confidence** and having made up one's mind are indicated by steepling.

Some in sales prefer to concentrate on getting new business (**hunters**) while others like to revisit clients regularly to maintain links (**gatherers**). Either way, long-term success depends upon the rapport struck up between seller and buyer, much of which has to do with mutual acceptance of each other's body talk.

4 Be cautious about playing the expert

Selling undoubtedly relies upon expertise, but you need to take care before playing the expert. You may know considerably more about the product than the buyer, but it's often better to play safe and first let the buyer display his or her knowledge of the subject.

Sometimes the buyer will convey a sense of 'giving way to' the seller's expertise, but this may be as much to 'test out' the substance of the seller's knowledge and experience as to learn about the product.

Noting tone of voice

Noting the buyer's tone of voice can make all the difference here. If, for example, the buyer says 'I see; tell me more', it might mean one of three things.

- 'I am interested; carry on.'
- 'I'll humour you for the moment, but I'm not convinced.'
- 'I don't believe you for a moment.'

The real meaning behind the buyer's questions lies in the tone of voice, not the words.

Your response to ambiguity of this kind needs to be positive and should seek to affirm what you have already been saying. Open body language is all-important here. You want to come across as confident and assertive, so:

- maintain eye contact
- smile (but don't grimace)
- keep an upright, open body stance
- remember that 'palms down' expresses certainty.

Whatever you do, have faith in yourself. There is nothing worse than looking down, as this suggests resignation or defeat. Equally, fidgeting can be seen as shiftiness and the client may lose trust in you.

If the buyer does not have the expertise and knowledge about the product or service and clearly indicates that you are the expert, here is your chance to adopt the **consultant style** of selling, where you solve their problems and difficulties as part of the sales process. The consultative style is shown by assertive gestures and postures and a confident tone of voice.

5 Be sincere; look the part

Successful salespeople tend to be outgoing, extrovert individuals. Some are genuinely charismatic and exude enthusiasm and charm and have little difficulty in securing the interest of their clients. Others work hard on their presentation skills to make up for any lack of spontaneity. In both cases, what makes them successful is their **sincerity**, and they achieve this by ensuring that their **body language is in synch with their words**.

Negotiating skills

In sales negotiations sellers have a price they want to sell at and a price they cannot go below. Buyers, on the other hand, have a price in mind that they want to buy at and a price they can't afford. Neither party wants the other to know their range of discretion, as this would give the game away.

During negotiations both parties use body language to signal their agreement, disagreement, interest, disinterest, surprise, pleasure, alarm, etc., adding a sense of drama to the process. Both watch carefully for chinks in the other's armour, the aim being to play their best 'hand' at the most opportune moment.

The selling game

As in a game of poker, sales negotiators do not want to give away too much in case they betray their positions. Some buyers will remain expressionless – **'poker faced'** – making it difficult for the sales person to establish rapport and to gauge what the buyer is thinking. Others **'play their cards close to the chest'**, indicating that they are not going to give anything away. **'Sitting on the fence'** gives the impression that a decision could go either way; **'stony faced'** suggests a hardening of position, which may not be in the seller's favour, while keeping a **'stiff upper lip'** implies keeping feelings under wraps so that intentions can't be read. It is only when **'all the cards are on the table'** and decisions have been taken that body language displays true feelings.

Push and pull

The body language you adopt during sales negotiations influences customer perceptions of your sincerity and ability to deliver. **Push** too hard and you will appear too demanding. **Pull** too early and you risk losing the catch (Ribbens & Whitear, 2007).

'**Push**' body language tends to be *assertive* and indicated by a forward posture, intense facial expressions, resonant voice, regular eye contact and directive hand gestures.

'**Pull**' body language tends to be *reactive*, involving relaxed and open body posture, expressive gestures, and friendly facial expressions and tone of voice.

'Push' and 'pull' styles reflect the difference between expecting compliance from clients and wanting to co-operate with them. When you *push*, you are effectively demanding that the other party complies with your bidding. When you *pull*, you are proposing a way forward that you think the client will find attractive. In practice, you are likely to use both, though over-reliance on either could limit your success.

Successful business negotiations involve a willingness to consider the needs of the client and an awareness of the limits to which you can go in achieving your objectives. If you appear indifferent, you will give the impression that the outcome doesn't matter to you. If you concede too much, you stand to lose the advantage. On the other hand, if you are prepared to bargain and co-operate, you stand a greater chance of fulfilling your own as well as the client's needs.

Skill in negotiating successfully lies in your preparedness to sacrifice lesser needs in order to secure more important ones. But how you 'come across' – your body language – is just as important as what you say.

Negative negotiating behaviour

- **Demanding** behaviour can produce quick results but it causes resentment and hostility in the longer term. Such behaviour includes aggressive body posture, harsh tone of voice, stern facial expressions, prolonged eye contact, invasion of personal space and exaggerated gestures.
- **Indifference** suggests a 'couldn't care less' attitude, implying that the issue is of little importance. Such behaviour includes laid-back body posture, disinterested facial expressions, limited gestures, lowered voice tone and little eye contact.
- **Conceding** behaviour suggests the person is prepared to give too much ground to the other party in order to demonstrate compliance. This would include defensive or appeasing gestures, apprehensive looks, limited eye contact and low voice tone.

Positive negotiating behaviour

- **Bargaining** body language is *flexible*. It is **assertive** when required, e.g. forward posture, strong facial expressions, tone of voice, gestures and eye contact; **relaxed** when *happy* to concede a point as part of a longer-term winning strategy, e.g. head nod, smile, shrug, hand wave.

- **Co-operative body language** is more pull than push, assertive yet *inclusive*, e.g. open posture and gestures, relaxed manner, designed to maintain rapport.

If your body language skills let you down, even the best negotiating skills are unlikely to help you succeed.

Body language in telephone selling

If you watch colleagues talking on the telephone, you'll notice that some of them *appear* to be in face-to-face contact with the person on the other end of the line. Their posture, gestures and tone of voice reflect their thoughts, and the more animated they become, the more they look as if they are *in touch* with the other person.

It may seem odd to say that adopting the wrong posture while on the telephone can give the wrong impression to the listener, but there is some truth in this. Body posture conveys information about the telephone caller. For example, some people lower their height slightly when talking to a superior on the phone.

The point is that most telephone communication is restricted to **paralinguistic cues**; what you think and how you feel are conveyed through **voice intonation**. It is how you **sound** at the other end that determines the type of reaction. The word 'phoney' actually derives from the sensation (first described during the early days of the telephone) of mistrusting the disembodied voice.

In the case of something like 'cold calling' it's essential that the salesperson sounds confident, friendly and enthusiastic, no matter how difficult this may be. The person at the other end of the line doesn't know you and, if you don't sound genuine and self-assured, you'll lose them straight away.

One way round this situation is to 'psych' yourself up in advance by deliberately adopting a **positive frame of mind** and an **assertive body posture** before starting the call. Not only will this make you **sound more self-assured**, but it will also make you feel more **confident**. Try the following.

- **Stand with your head up** as you speak rather than sitting slumped at a desk.
- **Smile** when you talk; it comes across in your voice.
- **Reflect the other person's speed and tone of voice.** Most of us do this automatically as it is a way of getting on to the same 'wavelength' as the client. Needless to say, if the client is aggressive, abrupt, or has a voice impediment, this could be self-defeating.
- **Tune in to the client's way of thinking.** As we saw on Sunday, people tend to 'think' in three main ways: sight, sound and feeling. By noting the kinds of *images* being utilized in the client's language, the salesperson can subtly alter his or her approach to suit the situation. This improves your chances of getting on the same wavelength.

The client's territory

When you enter the client's territory, you are almost certainly at a disadvantage and you may find yourself touching your cuffs or your watch as a mild **defence mechanism**. As a rule of thumb, it is advisable to arrive early and to avoid sitting down on the chairs and sofas provided in the reception area. This is because being seated lowers your position when shaking hands and making eye contact. Also, sitting down can give the impression of an over-casual attitude, lacking respect for the client's authority.

A mild defence mechanism

The buyer's office

Going into a client's territory is one thing, but entering the inner sanctum of their office is another. Since business is about buying and selling, and since we know that the seller needs to respect the buyer's status in order to give the right impression, body language now counts for a great deal.

- Standing too upright or too close to the client will come across as **pushy** or **aggressive**, so change your stance accordingly.
- Standing less than 2 ft (60 cm) away from your client is **too intimate**, and 9 ft (2.7 m) is **too impersonal**. The best distance is 2–4 ft (60–120 cm). (In some cultures closer proximity is acceptable, so be aware of cultural differences.)
- Be aware of **posture congruence** and interactional synchronizing: adopt similar body postures and gestures but do not deliberately copy, as this will come across as contrived. Probably the best method is to use **crossover mirroring**, whereby the seller imitates the buyer's hand gestures with head movements.
- Never adopt a more relaxed posture than the buyer; remember your **position power**.
- The desk is **intimate territory**, so get permission before you place your documents on it and be careful when leaning over it.
- Use **active listening** gestures, such as the head cock, or murmurs and nods of agreement.
- Maintain **eye contact** with the buyer to be seen as more honest, persuasive, informed and credible.
- Be aware of hand gestures. Remember that **palms up** indicates honesty or uncertainty, while **palms down** conveys certainty and assuredness.
- If the buyer has adopted the 'steepling' gesture, it may mean that he or she has come to a decision. It is important for the seller to mentally note what gestures and comments preceded 'steepling' as this indicates possible success or failure in the transaction.

Summary

Selling is the art of *communication*, not just persuasion. Since most communication is non-verbal, body language can make the difference between success and failure. Understanding the body language of your client and reflecting this in your own helps to create the rapport essential to successful business relationships.

Today we learned not to use body language as a *deliberate* aid to selling – that is *acting* – but to follow the five basic ground rules for success.

1 Remember who you are (position power).
2 Make the client feel comfortable (reward power).
3 Use subtle persuasion, not coercion (coercive power).
4 Be cautious about playing the expert (expert power).
5 Be sincere; look the part (charisma power).

We have seen that successful negotiating depends on how prepared we are to sacrifice lesser needs to secure more important ones. Body language and tone of voice during sales negotiations influence customer perceptions of our sincerity and ability to deliver. Whether we are on the phone or on the client's own territory, a positive frame of mind and assertive body language will make us *sound* more self-assured.

Fact-check [answers at the back]

1. Who holds the power in the sales situation?
   a) The seller ☐
   b) The buyer ☐
   c) Both buyer and seller in equal degrees ☐
   d) Neither; it's the service that counts ☐

2. When selling, how should you approach the buyer?
   a) Display subservience ☐
   b) Offer subtle rewards ☐
   c) Stand close to him or her ☐
   d) Rub your hands when interest is shown ☐

3. When you observe the buyer's body language, what should you do?
   a) Mirror it exactly to create rapport ☐
   b) Adopt different postures and gestures ☐
   c) Ignore it completely ☐
   d) Reflect, not copy it ☐

4. If the buyer is aggressive, what should you do?
   a) Still try to establish rapport ☐
   b) Mirror the aggression ☐
   c) Tell him or her their behaviour is inappropriate ☐
   d) Move on to another customer ☐

5. How is critical evaluation indicated?
   a) Folded arms and leaning back ☐
   b) Chin on one hand with finger pointing up over cheek ☐
   c) Hands clasped behind head, elbows out, leaning back ☐
   d) Hands together, finger tips touching ☐

6. What do we call salespeople who prefer new customer challenges?
   a) Gatherers ☐
   b) Prospects ☐
   c) Hunters ☐
   d) Charismatics ☐

7. For the best response, how should salespeople appear to clients?
   a) As experts ☐
   b) Relaxed and self-assured ☐
   c) Ambiguous ☐
   d) Manipulative ☐

8. What characterizes telephone selling?
   a) It excludes the use of body language ☐
   b) It reduces the impact of body talk on the message ☐
   c) It highlights the importance of paralinguistic cues and tone of voice ☐
   d) It denies the opportunity to establish rapport ☐

9. When entering a client's office, what should you remember to do?
a) Keep 2–4 ft (60–120 cm) between you ☐
b) Stand upright and close ☐
c) Display a more relaxed posture than the client ☐
d) Place your documents on the desk ☐

10. How do you show active listening when selling?
a) By replying to the customer's questions ☐
b) By asking the customer questions ☐
c) By going over your sales pitch ☐
d) By using head nods, head cocks and paralinguistic cues ☐

SUNDAY

MONDAY

TUESDAY

WEDNESDAY

THURSDAY

FRIDAY

SATURDAY

Truth
detectives

How good are you at spotting the signs of deception? Do you know when you are being taken for a ride? Is telling a white lie the same as lying?

Today you will learn what kinds of body language occur when people are lying. For example, difficulty in maintaining eye contact, shuffling the feet, licking the lips, drumming the fingers, perspiring and blushing all indicate *stress*, even if the words they are speaking don't. Deception 'leaks out' through non-verbal behaviour or body language.

Those who investigate the honesty of others need to be able to spot the telltale signs of deception without making it obvious they are doing so. They need to recognize the non-verbal 'signatures' of concealment, falsification and lying. The ability to spot inappropriate or 'out-of-place' body language is what enables security personnel to respond quickly to complex situations and to distinguish between those who pose a threat and those who do not.

Today you'll find out how to spot the clues and improve your ability to tell truth from lies. You'll also learn some basic rules for modifying your own body language so that you can become more effective at predicting, reducing and tackling conflict.

Uncovering deception

Paradoxically, people involved in deception usually try to avoid blatant lying (Comer et al., 1992). For example, they may:

- fail to answer a question asked
- pretend not to understand it
- remain silent
- feign emotion, such as anger
- pretend they are feeling ill.

If they can't get away with concealing what they are doing, they may then begin to falsify the situation by:

- inventing a scenario
- telling a tall story
- telling a lie.

To conceal or avoid telling **direct lies** often involves watering down one's statements. Richard Nixon's famous counter to the allegation that he authorized the 1972 Watergate break-in, 'The President would not do such a thing,' is a classic example of this. By depersonalizing the act – taking the 'I' out of the equation – he absolved himself of responsibility for it.

Stress – the body language of deception

> *'He that has eyes to see and ears to hear may convince himself that no mortal can keep a secret. If his lips are silent, he chatters with his fingertips. Betrayal oozes out of every pore.'*
>
> Sigmund Freud, 1905

The body language of stress gives us clues that certain individuals may be trying to conceal the truth. To place this in context, we need to consider the situation in which distinctive body movements and actions take place. For example, a yawn may just indicate tiredness, but in stressful circumstances it can indicate an intention to deceive.

Other indications of deception are:

- making odd facial expressions
- stretching
- avoiding eye contact
- pausing for longer than usual, or going silent
- exhibiting glazed expressions
- repeatedly clearing the throat
- making speech errors
- alternating the pitch of the voice
- grinding teeth or biting lips
- touching the nose.

In some cases, individuals under suspicion decrease their normal expressive hand and arm movements, using their hands instead to smoothe the nose, mouth and brow. 'Picking lint' is often observed in 'guilty' behaviour.

Anxiety associated with deceiving others can also have the following physiological effects:

- shortness of breath
- difficulty in swallowing
- dry mouth
- flushing or blanching of the face
- sweating and palpitations.

Lying signals

Research by Paul Ekman and colleagues in the Department of Psychiatry at the University of California has identified facial expressions, gestural slips and subtle speech signals that indicate when individuals are lying. Curiously, while successful observers can identify deception 80 per cent of the time, they recognize the truth only 66 per cent of the time. For this reason Ekman cautions that 'judging deception from facial expressions and body language will probably never be sufficiently accurate to be admissible in the courtroom'.

In extreme circumstances the liar's body can appear 'frozen', with arms and legs tightly folded in a defensive posture. Flushing, indicating a slight increase in skin temperature, is a key measure of lie detector testing in the USA.

Comer and his co-authors have suggested (1992) that subtle rewards and punishments should be used when making distinctions between perceived 'truths' and 'lies'. For example, if an interviewee appears to be speaking honestly, then:

- the response should be friendly and open, for example using the 'palms-up' gesture
- first names should be used
- the interviewer should look directly at, and smile at, the interviewee
- personal space can be increased between the two of them by leaning or moving back.

On the other hand, if the interviewee appears to be imparting something less than the truth, the response can be more confrontational. For example, the interviewer should:

- use gestures such as finger pointing
- gaze at the individual for slightly longer than usual or look away
- use the subject's surname rather than their first name
- lean forward to decrease their personal space.

The aim here is to counter the apparent deception and draw it out into the open.

Nose touching

It is well known that when people tell lies, or even hear other people lying, they tend to touch their noses. There seem to be two explanations for this gesture. Firstly, by touching the nose the hand covers the mouth where the lies are coming from – children cover their mouths when telling lies. Secondly, when people tell lies it causes stress, and stress causes the skin to get slightly hotter. When the skin gets hotter, the nose, which is a sensitive organ, may itch or even expand slightly (the so-called 'Pinocchio effect') so the individual touches the itching nose.

Clues, not evidence

A word of warning to the over-zealous: non-verbal communication provides *clues* to how people think and feel, not *evidence*. Just because someone appears nervous or behaves uncharacteristically does not prove wrongdoing.

Richard Wiseman's experiments (*Quirkology*, 2007) suggest that there is *no* visual evidence of body language in deliberate deception, since people observed *telling stories* or *acting* displayed none of the characteristics of lying. However, what this probably tells us is that the *portrayal* of deception is not the same thing as the *experience* of deceiving. Those who *know* they are not actually lying do not exhibit the stress signals associated with it.

Body language in security and control

Those who guard, control, observe or investigate, such as the police, security personnel and insolvency practitioners, are tasked with the responsibility of protecting the public. They have a helping function and yet their presence can appear threatening in certain circumstances. For those directly involved in security activities there is, therefore, a need to balance the perception of the **helping** function with that of **control**, particularly if the public is to view their services in a positive light.

In recent years, for example, armed police have maintained a presence at some of our major international airports. They have to be seen to be alert and professional, while remaining relatively inconspicuous. Were they to act inappropriately – leaning in doorways, chewing gum – they would undoubtedly alarm the very people they were sent to protect.

It is the ability to spot inappropriate or 'out-of-place' body language in others that enables security personnel to respond quickly to complex situations and to distinguish between those who pose a threat and those who do not. For example, the panic displayed by a mother losing sight of her child in a public place would not be interpreted as threatening, even though the body language of those involved might indicate high levels of anxiety and stress.

During one training course a female airport security officer reported that she had apprehended a woman who was carrying drugs strapped to her body. The woman looked pregnant but the security officer said that her suspicions were aroused because the suspect didn't have a 'pregnant face'. Such sensitivity to detail (*body talk*) has much to do with intuition, or having an 'experienced eye for the unexpected'.

Airport security – high stress, low tolerance

In his book *Manwatching*, Desmond Morris (1978) found that more verbal and physical aggression is exhibited at airports, railway stations, bus stations and ports than in most other public places. Airports, in particular, are subject to high levels of such **stress-related behaviour**. But why?

According to Morris, it is because travel, and especially air travel, is innately stressful. Just getting to the airport can be a nightmare, with the potential for traffic jams, detours, accidents, panic over missing the plane and things left behind.

The two most common causes of anxiety are fear of flying and loss of personal space.

● **Fear of flying**
   Morris found that people exhibit ten times as many signs of tension (displacement activities) at airports as at railway stations. Only 8 per cent of the passengers about to board a train showed these signs, but the figure rose to 80 per cent at the check-in desk of a jumbo jet flight.
● **Loss of personal space**
   Aggressive body language arises when people are forced to wait in queues, are crowded into restrictive spaces, or feel crammed into aeroplane seats.

The notion of 'personal space' is also culturally determined. In the USA and western Europe, 'one's own space' is anything under an arm's length; in Mediterranean cultures, it is under elbow length, while in eastern Europe it is about wrist length.

Given that people of all cultures regularly mix at airports, it means that levels of tolerance are bound to differ and clashes are highly likely to occur. When they do, those in the front line who are responsible for managing the public – immigration, customs and excise, police, security and airline personnel – have to deal with whatever arises while remaining polite, calm and in control.

Recognizing tension

Being able to recognize tension in others is a first step towards limiting confrontation and alleviating stress. Cabin crew are specially trained to watch for the telltale signs of tension, particularly among fidgeting passengers, which can include:

- repeatedly checking tickets or passports
- rearranging hand luggage
- dropping things
- constantly making 'vital last-minute checks'
- changing position in their seats
- grimacing
- head scratching
- earlobe tugging
- rubbing the back of the neck with the palm of the hand.

When tension cannot be **displaced** in these ways, it begins to spill over into aggressive behaviour. Sometimes this aggression may be **directed** at inanimate objects like airport furniture or expressed through actions like door slamming. At other times it may be **targeted** at airport staff verbally through argument and confrontation, or non-verbally in the form of aggressive body language.

Staff who find themselves at the centre of an 'incident' – for example, when a disagreement threatens to become physically aggressive – may, quite simply, have been insensitive to the moods and feelings of those they are dealing with.

When this happens, the following can occur:

- raised voices
- pointing
- rolling one's eyes in frustration
- standing too close.

It has been observed that some security staff tend to be involved in more 'incidents' than others. This is often because their body language, tone of voice or other mannerism makes them 'incident prone'. By not being aware of how these factors can contribute to a situation they inadvertently escalate the problem.

Ambiguous gestures

One of the problems with the gestures that people use when they are anxious, angry, frightened or feeling belligerent is that these gestures can mean different things to different people, depending on their ethnic or cultural background. What may be insulting in one country might not be in another, and what might be considered a light-hearted gesture to some can be offensive to others.

In Saudi Arabia, for example, touching the lower eyelid with the forefinger indicates stupidity, whereas in other cultures the same gesture implies 'secrecy' or disbelief. Tapping or twisting the forefinger against the temple is a variant of the stupidity gesture, but since in some cultures it also implies that you have a screw loose or that your brain is addled, misinterpretation can easily result in aggressive counter-reaction.

Similarly, the Greek *Moutza*, in which an open hand is thrust towards another person, meaning 'get lost', means 'stop there' to police and security officers in the UK. Another 'get lost!' gesture that causes problems if incorrectly interpreted is the 'chin-flick', which is when the back of the fingers are swept upward and forward against the underside of the chin. Desmond Morris points out that this gesture means 'get lost' in France and northern Italy but in southern Italy it means 'no' or 'I don't want any.'

Predicting conflict

The following gestures that exemplify aggressive behaviour can be useful predictors of potential conflict situations:

- **shaking the fist** at someone to express contempt
- **the hand chop or hand slice,** where the hand is used like an axe to suggest execution
- **prodding with the fingertips** in the direction of another person's eyes
- **finger pointing**, less aggressive than prodding, but still threatening
- **staring or 'eyeballing'** – as boxers do before a fight – in order to intimidate or control a situation
- **crowding** or invading someone's personal space.

It goes without saying that exerting pressure in this way can be interpreted as coercive. Standing in close proximity to someone, for example, has long been known as a means of exerting pressure on someone by raising their stress level. Such techniques used by those in authority can escalate a situation, and therefore it is important to approach such a scenario with sensitivity and care. For those in security who need to gain someone's attention, for example, it is better to use the whole hand to point rather than the forefinger.

Predicting violence

Fortunately, most threats of aggression do not result in physical violence, as people generally prefer to avoid injury. For those involved in security and crowd management it is wise to note the precursors to actual violence, the non-verbal signals betrayed by body language. The first of these is **adrenalizing**, the symptoms of which Desmond Morris has described as 'the cold sweat of fear'.

1 As the body's **fight-or-flight mechanism** kicks into action, adrenalin pumps round the system in preparation for action.
2 When this happens, breathing tends to speed up and deepen, face tone pales, sweating occurs, shivering begins, the mouth begins to feel dry and the individual starts to lick his lips and swallow.

3 As the nervous system gears up for action, posture begins to alter. The body's response to signals of danger is 'squaring up', making it appear **ready for combat**.
4 The eyes narrow, the mouth widens, shoulders are raised and the neck and head are thrust forward. The arms bend slightly and the fists begin to clench. As the trunk pushes outward, the abdomen contracts and the knees bend to give them more 'spring' in order to be able to defend as well as attack.

Avoiding confrontation

To be able to resolve confrontational or threatening situations you need to follow certain basic rules.

● Be assertive, not confrontational
Problems are rarely solved through confrontation or argument.

● Remain calm
Try to ensure that your own body language is neither defensive nor threatening. You need to be seen to be in control.

● Keep the aggressor at arm's length
This allows you to step aside should the individual lunge at you. Avoid touching or grabbing someone who is angry as this will only encourage retaliation.

You can always tell if you are getting too close to someone: they will usually step or lean back, or fold their arms in a defensive posture.

● Don't condescend
Avoid using a tone of voice or gestures that could be interpreted as 'talking down to' a person, implying that they are stupid. This is more likely to inflame than calm the situation. People are not stupid; they may be angry, confused, slow, muddled or even disabled in some way.

Don't shout or raise your voice

Shouting is an aggressive way of communicating and is likely to annoy not only the person you are dealing with, but also others around you.

Don't point

If you want someone's attention, or you wish to direct them in a certain way, use your whole hand. Pointing directly at individuals, and even pointing with the thumb, nodding or tossing your head in a certain direction are regarded as surly gestures and are likely to cause irritation.

Don't beckon with the forefinger only

This is often perceived as demeaning or sarcastic. It is better to use your whole hand, rolling the fingers towards you with the palms up, although in Italy, Spain, South America, Africa and Asia the same gesture is used but with the palms face down. When dealing with children or large groups, it is acceptable to use the whole arm to beckon, but slowly so as to avoid the impression of rushing people. You may have noticed that tour guides and the military raise the whole arm above their heads while rotating the forefingers, meaning 'come around me'.

Retain eye contact

This shows the other person that you are interested and concerned. Looking down or away may be construed as lack of interest and cause annoyance.

Avoid dissent

This means trying not to shake your head or wag your finger. If you need to say no, it is better to use the whole-hands, palms-down gesture while at the same time maintaining friendly eye contact.

Maintain an upright posture when sitting

This will appear attentive, professional and lacking in tension. Slouching, hanging your legs over a chair or putting your feet on a desk appears disrespectful; leaning back with your hands clasped behind your head and elbows sticking out looks 'superior'.

● Avoid 'picking lint'

The effect of this gesture is to indicate that you are not in agreement with someone but you can't be bothered to argue with them.

● Show understanding

When the person you are dealing with is getting flustered, simple gestures such as patting the palms in a gentle, downward motion, combined with comments such as 'I understand your feelings, so let's talk about it', can make a difficult situation less confrontational. The age-old tradition of offering tea or coffee at such times might also not go amiss.

Follow these basic rules and you will become far more effective in identifying stress and deception as well as tackling conflict and reducing confrontation.

Summary

Today you learned how the *body language of stress* offers clues about whether an individual may be trying to conceal the truth. Since certain kinds of body language occur more often when people are lying than when they are telling the truth, we can learn to spot the clues, and find out whether someone is lying.

Deception 'leaks out' when someone fails to control their body language, and being able to identify this 'out-of-place' body language enables security personnel to identify potential threats and apprehend offenders before situations get out of control.

When stress and tension cannot be displaced they quickly spill over into aggression. This is more likely to occur at airports, railway stations, bus stations and ports than in other public places. Staff and crew are adept at predicting potential conflict by understanding body language such as fist shaking, prodding, pointing, eyeballing and crowding.

By learning some simple rules about modifying our own body language in stressful situations, we can all become more effective at reducing and tackling conflict.

SUNDAY

MONDAY

TUESDAY

WEDNESDAY

THURSDAY

FRIDAY

SATURDAY

Fact-check [answers at the back]

1. What do people intent on deliberate deception tend to do?
a) Avoid blatant lying ☐
b) Happily lie through their teeth ☐
c) Have no problem answering questions ☐
d) Believe they are telling the truth ☐

2. When people are lying, what do they tend to do?
a) Sit on their hands ☐
b) Look relaxed ☐
c) Maintain eye contact ☐
d) Avoid eye contact ☐

3. What distinguishes liars from storytellers?
a) Different kinds of body language ☐
b) Liars exhibit stress reactions ☐
c) Storytellers show signs of stress ☐
d) Nothing; both are as bad as each other ☐

4. What do lie detector tests in the USA measure?
a) Hand and arm movements ☐
b) Pulse ☐
c) Skin temperature ☐
d) Facial expressions ☐

5. What should you do if you suspect a person is lying in an interview?
a) Use his or her surname and lean forwards ☐
b) Lean back and use his or her first name ☐
c) Look directly at him or her and smile ☐
d) Pretend you are hearing the truth ☐

6. What does covering your nose and mouth with your hand suggest?
a) You can't face talking to someone ☐
b) Your nose is cold ☐
c) You are lying ☐
d) You are embarrassed ☐

7. How much of the time can a well-trained observer identify liars?
a) 20 per cent ☐
b) 40 per cent ☐
c) 60 per cent ☐
d) 80 per cent ☐

8. What are airports, railway stations and docks ideal for?
a) Practising deception ☐
b) Witnessing stressed behaviour ☐
c) Maintaining personal space ☐
d) Relaxing ☐

9. In what circumstances does stress 'leak out' in body language?
a) When people aren't telling the truth ❏
b) When people feel their personal space threatened ❏
c) When people need another cup of coffee ❏
d) When people feel intimidated ❏

10. How can security staff avoid conflict?
a) By keeping stressed people at arm's length ❏
b) By raising their voices to show who's in control ❏
c) By beckoning with the forefinger ❏
d) By looking down and picking fluff off their clothes ❏

SUNDAY
MONDAY
TUESDAY
WEDNESDAY
THURSDAY
FRIDAY
SATURDAY

SATURDAY

Active listening

Every good manager knows that the aim of face-to-face interviews – whether for selection and appraisal, coaching or counselling – is to encourage the interviewee to do most of the talking. This means that the person conducting the interview should be an active listener as well as a questioner. But listening means more than simply hearing the words. Being receptive to the cues that people give through their body language is just as important.

Active listening involves using two important skills:

● being aware of your own body language and paralinguistic cues to show that you are attentive to what the other person is saying
● noting the signals and cues that they are giving you so that you understand the real meanings and feelings behind their words.

Working with people's feelings is a skill that some of us perform more naturally than others. A common mistake in such situations is to confuse giving advice with counselling. You can be a good listener, you can be empathetic and encouraging, and you can come up with solutions to surface problems, but you may not actually recognize the underlying causes of the problems or be able to deal with their unexpected consequences.

The face-to-face interview

Are you a good listener? You may think you are, but listening is more than simply hearing words. Being receptive to the cues that interviewees give through their body language is just as important. As a rule of thumb, aim to ensure that your interviewee does the talking for about 75 per cent of the time during selection and appraisal and up to 90 per cent of the time during counselling.

First impressions

In selection interviewing, for example, how interviewee and interviewer initially perceive each other can determine the outcome of the selection process. If the interviewer just sits there with an expressionless face, giving little indication of interest in, or reaction to, the interviewee, the chances are that the interviewee will 'clam up' and fail to make the best of him- or herself.

People in interviews are usually nervous and will tend to talk freely, openly and honestly only when they begin to feel a rapport with the interviewer. This is why interviewers need to be careful not to prejudge the person before them on the basis of first impressions.

Initial judgements are always speculative, and for this reason you need to be aware of your own prejudices, particularly relating to social class, gender, ethnic background, dress and appearance, before making judgements. The word prejudice, *after all, means to prejudge, and it's imperative not to prejudge the outcome of an interview before you've really started.*

Research has shown that we tend to make judgements about people when we first meet them: we assess their personality, intelligence, temperament, attractiveness, friendliness and so on. Sometimes intuition informs us, but this isn't enough to draw conclusions – it merely gives a *sense* of what a person is like without actually knowing why.

There are some simple rules for neutralizing **first impression bias**.

- Be prepared to recognize your own prejudices and make allowances for them.
- Remember that assumptions are not facts and do not constitute evidence.
- Treat each interviewee similarly and try to ask the same questions (so that you can make an objective comparison between candidates).

Getting comfortable

Getting people to relax at the start of an interview is important, as they tend to be more open and honest if they feel at ease. Don't begin the process by sitting behind a desk, as this tends to create a **physical**, and therefore a **psychological**, **barrier**. It is often better to sit on low chairs round a coffee table or opposite each other using the corner of a table, as this creates a more relaxed atmosphere.

'There's something about this candidate I don't trust.'

Breaking the ice

As the interviewer, make your initial questions informal, in order to encourage a natural dialogue. For example, you might want to approach a counselling session obliquely in order to reduce possible tension by asking simply and with a smile: 'Have you done this before? Don't worry, it's easy', followed by (a palms-up) 'How can I help?'

In most interview situations, don't:

- start off with an accusatory tone of voice or remark
- lean too far forward – it's aggressive
- point – this is also aggressive
- sit back with arms and legs crossed – this shows defensiveness
- lean back, hands behind head – this conveys superiority.

If you appear aggressive, too formal or superior, you will delay getting to know each other and give the other person less of a chance to participate effectively. You may even witness their **physical retreat** as they fold their arms and legs defensively.

Active listening and body language

If you want people to talk freely, you have to 'actively listen'. This means **responding non-verbally in ways that encourage rapport.** Ways to do this include:

- tilting the head to one side to show that you are listening with interest
- nodding your head slowly to show you understand and are willing to continue listening
- smiling and using small hand movements as encouragement to continue speaking
- using 'hmms' and murmurs of approval where relevant
- raising an eyebrow slightly if something sparks interest, or even more if you are amazed or cannot agree.

These are body language modes of encouragement, essential to maintaining the subject's flow of conversation. It doesn't matter what form the interview takes; the aim is to show that you **understand** and that you are **taking in** what is being said. You are *not trying to declare your own position* either in terms of your own views, or expressing emotions such as pleasure, displeasure, agreement, disagreement or alarm. At this stage you simply want the other party to relax and communicate with you.

Some managers are so intent upon conveying a 'neutral' or 'professional' approach that they conduct interviews as if they are playing poker – expressionless and still. But if you don't smile, nod or provide other paralinguistic forms of encouragement, your neutral body language may well be self-defeating: the interviewee will stop talking.

Making notes

During selection and appraisal interviews you should be making brief notes. Don't be tempted to rest your notepad on a table, however, since this will cause you to look down and, thereby, break eye contact. The interviewee will often interpret this as time to stop talking, so it is better to use a clipboard on your knee so as to maintain the eyeline.

Relaxed posture, easy rapport

If neither of you is relaxed, you will not get the best out of the interview situation. Watch out for **defensive postures** such as:

● leaning back
● arms folded, ankles crossed
● tense smile.

Research indicates that unrelaxed postures not only reflect but also create tension. Most of us know that smiling makes us feel better; so, too, does a relaxed posture. In fact, it helps us to **open up mentally**. Awareness of your own body language can actually make you think and feel differently.

There are various ways to encourage relaxation. Having tea or coffee not only sets an informal tone, but will also stop the interviewee from adopting a closed or defensive posture and hence a defensive frame of mind. Try drinking tea or coffee when sitting down with your arms and legs crossed – it's not possible.

When counselling an employee, look for the postures that suggest a negative frame of mind, such as:

- drooping shoulders
- lack of eye contact
- sullen appearance
- looking down
- self-protective 'wrapping', in which the arms are folded on the chest
- nervous fidgeting and position changing.

'I'm okay – nothing wrong with me.'

Dealing with sensitive issues in appraisal

If you need to give someone constructive feedback (a better term than criticism), it is important to be **assertive** but **non-threatening**.

- You need to start off on the *right foot*, to use a body language expression. The best approach is to start with the individual's strengths or merits and then introduce your concerns. This approach is more likely to deter defensiveness and will encourage your appraisee to relax enough to be able to listen to your concerns.
- It is essential to avoid words, gestures and voice tones that imply criticism, particularly suggestions of weakness or failure.

Your objective is to **communicate**, not to criticize. Being too clever is a recipe for disaster. Saying things like 'Don't worry, it can't get any worse', 'You've reached rock bottom', or 'You'll have to dig yourself out of that one' do nothing to solve the problem.

Appraisers have to be sensitive to their own body language as well as that of the appraisee. Managers with these extra interpersonal skills are more likely to end the appraisal process with motivated employees than with depressed and demotivated ones.

Maintaining rapport

The manager's job is, equally, not to interrogate the interviewee, but to **facilitate** the communication process. Having established rapport, how do you then maintain it?

'Getting on' with someone involves synchronizing our responses with the other person to some extent. We all do it, often without realizing. The NLP experts Joseph O'Connor and John Seymour (1994) go as far as to argue that rapport involves matching and mirroring body language and tonality. This doesn't mean copying another person's behaviour, but showing in subtler ways that you are, so to speak, on the same wavelength.

- You can use **crossover mirroring** – the matching of an arm movement with a small hand movement, or a shift in posture with a corresponding movement of the head. This emphasizes that you are in sympathy with the other person.
- You can show sensitivity to the words the other person uses by **reflecting back** the same kind of language, as explained on Sunday when we described how people think in different ways – in terms of sight, sound and feeling.
- At the other end of the spectrum, changes in facial expression, tone of voice and unlocking of the hands can make it equally clear that you are **disengaging** from the conversation.

Touching
One of the more contentious issues to do with maintaining rapport concerns actual physical contact, or touching.

In the UK and USA, touching work colleagues, especially subordinates, is far less common than on the European mainland and in some cases is frowned upon. This is a pity because the simple gesture of touching someone to show support, encouragement, agreement or gratitude tends to be received with warmth, thereby reinforcing rapport. Sometimes it is positively helpful to touch someone, as after difficult appraisal or counselling sessions when reaching out a hand to lightly touch an employee's arm, shoulder or back can only be construed as a **gesture of support**.

Among people of the same sex, a pat on the back – preferably the shoulder blades – by a more senior manager is also likely to be seen as a form of **reward**. Indeed, it can be a highly significant gesture, as the expression 'I was touched when she thanked me' indicates.

It has also been observed that people are more likely to touch others when giving information or advice, which suggests that touching is a type of **reinforcement** of what is being said. Similarly, we touch each other when asking a favour rather than granting one, or when listening to other people's worries rather than them listening to ours. It's as if we're saying, 'We are friends, so can you help me out with...?' or 'I understand. Tell me about it.'

Fact or fiction?

Yesterday we talked about uncovering deception in security situations, where the concern is deliberate concealment and falsification. In appraisal and counselling you more often find people **in denial** or being 'economical with the truth', covering up for their weaknesses and failures.

In the selection interview the one thing that the interviewer needs to know for sure is whether the interviewee is telling the truth about qualifications, experience and skills. Asking for documentary evidence and references is a partial way of checking someone's honesty, but face-to-face interviews can help you distinguish fact from fiction.

In a survey of 1,500 companies it was found that 71 per cent had encountered serious lying on CVs. Of the most common,

31 per cent concerned previous experience, 21 per cent university qualifications, 19 per cent salary and 18 per cent secondary qualifications (Experian Survey, January 2000).

Uncomfortable truths

The astute manager may well be able to pick up hints of deception and self-deception by observing body language. Sometimes it is as if the body is telling a different story from the one the words are conveying. Take the case of what we call 'uncomfortable truths'.

In the counselling situation, you **encourage** rather than press the individual to open up and, in the process, you may come across a problem that is **masked** by the reaction described. Even if there is an 'uncomfortable truth' involved here, what you don't do is put pressure on the person to talk. Sensitivity to what is going on 'behind the scenes' is all-important.

Uncovering a problem

You come across an issue during the course of discussion, and you follow it up with a question in order to gain clarity. However, instead of the straightforward answer that you expect, the interviewee **goes silent**. You press further and you get an **exaggerated response** – a **shifting of position**, **crossed arms**, attempts to **avert your gaze**. When you suggest that the issue is perhaps not quite as clear as was first assumed, the interviewee vehemently **denies** that the situation occurred, or **argues** that it cannot be construed in the way that you are describing it. What do you do?

If you press much harder, the chances are that you will lose rapport altogether. The point here is whether or not you have found out what you were looking for. In selection and appraisal you would undoubtedly have touched upon a weakness or a concealment of some kind.

Taking the strain

During face-to-face interviews the perceptive manager should be able to identify the stressed employee. This is especially important during an appraisal or a counselling session. When people are under too much pressure at work, it tends to show in their moods, body language and ability to cope with everyday tasks.

Stress is a natural state of readiness for action but, when it becomes too much, **strain** occurs and the body displays symptoms of not coping adequately. This is more likely to happen among people with limited control over their working lives, which is why it is incumbent upon the manager **to identify staff who are stressed in this way**.

In many cases, stressed individuals are **less aware** of their symptoms than those around them because the inability to cope builds up over time. Examples of body language typical of work-related stress are:

- hypersensitivity to mild criticism
- rejection of helpful advice
- displaying tense postures
- showing irritation by shrugging shoulders, 'tutting' or casting eyes to the ceiling.

If the problems are closer to the surface, the affected individual may:

- appear restless
- tremble
- exhibit nervous laughter or incoherent speech.

Physical symptoms of stress include:

- tense muscles
- indigestion
- increased heart rate
- nausea
- aches, pains or twitches

- appetite changes
- sleep problems
- exhaustion.

Being able to read and understand **pressure signals** is essentially a matter of experience. During interviews it is always worth noting **signs of discomfort** as these may indicate that something is wrong. As mentioned previously, *false yawns, artificial smiles, hand rubbing, picking lint, averting one's eyes* and *fidgeting* are all common indicators of stressed behaviour.

The body language of strain

To the experienced eye, the body language of strain is not difficult to detect. The slight **stoop** of the depressed person, the recurring **backache** of the overloaded employee, the **hangdog look** of the defeated colleague and the **distracted glances** of the anxious supervisor are all indicative of problems that are failing to be identified or alleviated.

The sympathetic touch

Working with people's feelings is a skill that some people perform more naturally than others. Learning such skills often requires you to **get in touch** with feelings that lie beneath the surface and come out only through posture, gesture and tone of voice.

Being a good listener, however, doesn't necessarily mean that you can recognize the underlying causes of problems or are in a position to deal with their consequences. It's a mistake to confuse **advice giving** with **counselling.** While you may be able to provide solutions to surface problems, tackling deeper issues is best left to qualified personnel.

If, as a manager, you find that an interview – particularly over disciplinary issues – is turning into a counselling session, you will need to change your approach. This may involve referral to a counsellor.

Dealing with emotional turmoil

If you do proceed with counselling someone yourself, you will probably find that you are dealing with one or more of the three main causes of emotional turmoil: **guilt, loss and failure**.

One of these may be relatively simple to unravel but, in combination, they can pose a considerable problem in terms of management. Sometimes getting to the source of a problem is made difficult because it is masked by **anger** on the one hand and **fear** on the other. Only sensitive probing will enable you to gain the confidence of the individual in question to talk about how they feel.

'The most precious gift we can offer anyone is our attention.'

Thich Nhat Hanh

The signs of stress: body language

It is essential to note the body language of over-expressive, anxious and 'unfulfilled' behaviour:

- the tautness of anger
- the hangdog look of unhappiness
- the hunched, burdened look
- the listless, depressed colleague
- the shrunken posture of failure
- the darting eyes of guilt
- the wracked expression of loss
- the hollow-eyed look of fear.

The signs of stress: verbal cues

It is equally essential to note the verbal cues that people give you – language that expresses physical or psychosomatic ailments. These cues can sometimes be a guide to the cause of the stress a person is suffering at work.

Ailment	Verbal cue
Backache	Lack of support
Laryngitis	Speechlessness
Stomach trouble	'Not being able to stomach' something
Tension headaches	Pressure
Breathlessness	Fear of performing badly
Blurred vision	Panic, or loss of perspective

Many physical conditions that we might never think of in terms of emotions have directly similar parallels. Once you have gained the **insight** into these issues and the **skills** to deal with them effectively, they will become **natural** to you and you will find that people increasingly relax in your company.

Summary

Today you have learned about the important skill of active listening. In interview situations, active listening means responding non-verbally in ways that encourage rapport. The manager's role is to facilitate the communication process, and your body language should demonstrate that you are taking in what is being said, not declaring your own position. This means ensuring that the interviewee does most of the talking, and that you are sensitive to their body language and the words they use. This indicates to them that you are *on the same wavelength*.

By recognizing your personal prejudices and treating interviewees equally, you avoid 'first impression bias' and so are able to make objective comparisons. Through observing body language you can spot when an interviewee is being 'economical with the truth' or is in denial about their weaknesses and failures. When body language 'tells a different story from the words being used', it may be betraying 'uncomfortable truths'.

Strain is when the body exhibits symptoms of not coping. Being able to identify pressure signals and signs of discomfort is an essential part of the manager's role.

Fact-check [answers at the back]

1. In a selection interview, how much time should the manager spend asking questions?
   a) 75 per cent ☐
   b) 60 per cent ☐
   c) 50 per cent ☐
   d) 25 per cent ☐

2. How can you avoid 'first impression bias'?
   a) Make assumptions about the interviewee and stick to them ☐
   b) Ask different candidates different questions ☐
   c) Recognize your own prejudices and make allowances for them ☐
   d) Remain silent and let the interviewee do the talking ☐

3. During selection and appraisal what should a manager do?
   a) Be an active listener and appear interested ☐
   b) Lean forward to indicate attentiveness ☐
   c) Sit back with arms and legs crossed ☐
   d) Lean back with hands behind the head ☐

4. How should a manager indicate agreement?
   a) Use rapid head nods ☐
   b) Use slow head nods ☐
   c) Maximize eye contact ☐
   d) Remain 'poker faced' ☐

5. What does offering tea or coffee in interviews help to do?
   a) Relax interviewees so that they 'open up' ☐
   b) Reinforce the manager's authority ☐
   c) Demonstrate the manager's social skills ☐
   d) Allow the manager to ask more questions ☐

6. What do people do when they are covering something up or indicating that something is wrong?
   a) Maintain eye contact ☐
   b) Start picking lint from their clothes ☐
   c) Look down and droop their shoulders ☐
   d) Steeple their hands ☐

7. What should a manager do with concerns about an individual's performance?
   a) Get directly to the point ☐
   b) Point out failures and weaknesses ☐
   c) Point out concerns before merits ☐
   d) Describe merits before concerns ☐

8. What is the purpose of crossover mirroring (using similar 'body talk')?
   a) To help maintain rapport ☐
   b) To show the manager's lack of sympathy ☐
   c) To indicate disagreement ☐
   d) To signal disengagement from a discussion ☐

9. What is the reason for touching someone on the arm or hand when giving advice?
a) Getting them to calm down ☐
b) Offering a gesture of support ☐
c) Stopping them disagreeing ☐
d) Demonstrating your power over them ☐

10. What does hypersensitivity to mild criticism or helpful advice, tense posture and restlessness suggest?
a) Irritability about being singled out ☐
b) An aggressive personality ☐
c) Being a bit under stress ☐
d) Experiencing strain and not coping properly ☐

Body words glossary

Sometimes the words and expressions we use to describe how we feel echo our states of mind, offering *verbal* confirmation of our body talk. This table gives some examples.

Body language term	State of mind
Laid back	Relaxed/comfortable
In a cold sweat	Anxiety/fear
Jumpy	Nervous
Squaring up to	Confrontational
Pinned down	Under pressure
Looking down one's nose at	Superiority
Touching a nerve	Irritation
If looks could kill	Hatred
That rings a bell	Recall
I hear what you say	Non-committal
Music to my ears	Satisfaction
Curling the lip	Aggression
Glazed expression	Boredom/confusion
Raised eyebrows	Surprise/indignation
In the palm of my hands	Manipulative/in control
Tight-lipped	Protective/defensive
Speechless	Shocked
Poker-faced	Calculating
Wrapped up in oneself	Preoccupied
Unable to stomach something	Repulsed
I'm really touched by that	Gratitude
Hollow-faced	Empty/haunted
Down in the mouth	Depressed
Seeing eye-to-eye	In harmony

Body language term	State of mind
Feel it in my bones	Certainty
Thick skinned	Well defended
Pain in the neck	Aggravation
To have your nose in front	Confidence
Nose out of joint	Compromised
Having considerable standing	Respect
Bent	Untrustworthy
Lose face	Lowered estimation
Facts at your fingertips	Authoritative
Towering	Powerful
Upright	Honest/dependable
Taking a dim view of	Critical
Needing breathing space	Claustrophobic

How many more can you add?

Bibliography

Comer, M. J., Price, D. H. & Ardis, P., *Bad Lies in Business* (New York: McGraw-Hill, 1992)

Experian Survey, *The Guardian*, 15 January 2000

French, J. R. & Raven, B., 'The causes of social power', in Cartwright, D. & Zander, A., (eds), *Group Dynamics* (London: Tavistock Publications, 1968)

Hay, J., *The Sunday Times*, 15 September 1996

Leech, T., *Winning Presentations*, 3rd edition (San Diego: Presentation Press, 2004)

Morris, D., *Manwatching* (London: Grafton Books, 1978)

O'Connor, J. & Seymour, J., *Introducing Neuro-Linguistic Programming* (London: Thorsons, 2003)

O'Connor, J. & Seymour, J., *Training with NLP* (London: Thorsons, 1994)

Ribbens, G. & Whitear G., *Body Language* (London: Hodder Arnold, 2007)

Wainwright, G. & Thompson, R., *Understand Body Language* (London: Hodder Headline, 2010)

Wiseman, R., *Quirkology: the Curious Science of Everyday Lives* (Macmillan, 2007)

Surviving in tough times

When times are tough, jobs are on the line and results matter more than ever. As a manager, your understanding of body language will help you look beyond what people say to what they really mean. Improving your ability to spot non-verbal clues will make you not only a better *active listener* but also a more effective communicator and leader. An awareness of other people's body language and careful use of your own will give you a *competitive advantage*: you will be seen to be more effective than others in all aspects of your working life. Here are ten key body language tips that will enhance your skill as a manager.

1 Encourage improved performance

The best managers are those who listen, not those who dictate or bully. Understanding body language enables you to tune into the thoughts and feelings of colleagues, which will build trust, helping to raise morale and make them more effective. By improving your communication skills you encourage others to perform at a higher level, which in turn will show you, as their manager or team leader, in the best light.

2 Gain insight into meanings and feelings

An awareness of body language allows you greater insight into the real meanings and feelings behind what people say. Body language may give you only clues, but careful observation can reinforce these clues and lead you to an understanding of people's real concerns. You can even use your awareness of body language to gain awareness of fraud, concealment and self-deception.

3 Increase your power and influence

You can spot those who have power and influence by their body language and you can increase *your* power and influence by your body language. It is not what you say but the way that you say it! It is your body language that conveys confidence, authority and even expertise. A submissive person may use the same words as you but their body language will still make them come across as submissive and they will be ignored – while you are listened to because of how you present yourself.

4 Enhance your authority

Inappropriate body language can be insulting or annoying. Coming across as too forceful or too relaxed can be offensive and mean that your message is ignored. Using appropriate body language, particularly in situations where you are dealing with valued clients or subordinates, can enhance the impact of your message. The right gesture or posture at the right time will increase your authority so that people will pay attention to your words.

5 Develop your presentation skills

Every presentation you make is essentially a *performance*, in which the hearts and minds of the audience are there to be won over. Since 90 per cent of the meaning of what we communicate is transmitted non-verbally, a large part of that performance relies upon *presence* rather than words. In addition, do not forget to tune into the body language of the audience; this will make your presentation much more effective.

6 Sell yourself

Selling is a *service*, which means respecting the buyer's needs. Push too hard and you can appear too demanding. Pull too early and you risk losing the catch. Appear too ingratiating and you'll come across as insincere or manipulative, too humble and you'll appear subservient. Remember that understanding body language will give you a sales advantage over others.

7 Spot the signs of deception

When someone's not telling the truth their body language can give them away. Signs of deception include avoiding eye contact, shuffling the feet, licking the lips, drumming the fingers, perspiring and blushing. Being able to spot the clues will help you to tell truth from lies and will help you realize when people are hiding things from you.

8 Recognize stress and strain

Hard economic times mean that people come under extra pressure. When stress becomes excessive, strain occurs and the body signals difficulties in coping, even when sufferers can't or won't talk about it. Managers need to be able to spot these signals early on and act sympathetically to deal with sensitive issues and alleviate undue distress.

9 Demonstrate positive leadership

You can be more effective as a leader if you exercise expert power and reward power. In many ways it is your body language that reinforces these two types of power, or influence, over others. The right body language reinforces your knowledge and expertise, and your team members will be motivated and feel rewarded by the right gesture and tone of voice from you: a smile, a handshake or a pat on the back are all elements of body language that 'touch' people.

10 Build rapport in interviews

Whether you are being interviewed for a job or promotion yourself or conducting a selection interview, an understanding of body language gives you an advantage. The competitive advantage comes from how you come across through your gestures, postures and facial expressions as well as your tone of voice. It is body language that helps you establish rapport: the 'taken-for-granted' world of non-verbal communication is what gives you the 'edge' over others. And when you are conducting an interview this skill will enable you look beyond mere words and understand what the interviewee really means.

Answers

Sunday: 1b; 2b; 3c; 4a; 5d; 6b; 7c; 8a; 9c; 10c.
Monday: 1b; 2c; 3a; 4d; 5b; 6d; 7d; 8a; 9d; 10c.
Tuesday: 1d; 2b; 3b; 4b; 5d; 6c; 7b; 8d; 9b; 10c.
Wednesday: 1c; 2b; 3c; 4b; 5d; 6a; 7d; 8b; 9b; 10c.

Thursday: 1b; 2b; 3d; 4a; 5b; 6c; 7b; 8c; 9a; 10d.
Friday: 1a; 2d; 3b; 4c; 5a; 6c; 7d; 8b; 9a; 10a.
Saturday: 1d; 2c; 3a; 4a; 5a; 6c; 7d; 8a; 9b; 10d.

ALSO AVAILABLE IN THE 'IN A WEEK' SERIES

For information about other titles in the series, please visit www.inaweek.co.uk

ALSO AVAILABLE IN THE 'IN A WEEK' SERIES

For information about other titles in the series, please visit www.inaweek.co.uk

LEARN IN A WEEK,
WHAT THE EXPERTS
LEARN IN A LIFETIME

For information about other titles
in the series, please visit
www.inaweek.co.uk

in

search

of

failure

Lessons from
The UK's Most Committed No-Hoper

BEN BYRAM-WIGFIELD

NEW HOLLAND

First published in 2004 by
New Holland Publishers (UK) Ltd
London • Cape Town • Sydney • Auckland
www.newhollandpublishers.com

Garfield House
86–88 Edgware Road
London W2 2EA, United Kingdom

80 McKenzie Street
Cape Town 8001, South Africa

Level 1, Unit 4
Suite 411, 14 Aquatic Drive
Frenchs Forest, NSW 2086, Australia

218 Lake Road
Northcote, Auckland, New Zealand

2 4 6 8 10 9 7 5 3 1

ISBN 1 84330 856 8

Senior Editor: Clare Sayer
Design: Paul Wright
Production: Hazel Kirkman
Editorial Direction: Rosemary Wilkinson

Printed and bound by Times Offset (M) Sdn Bhd, Malaysia

DISCLAIMER
The Author and The Publishers and its Agents and Vendors accept no
responsibility whatsoever for any ill health, injuries or fatalities arising from,
or related to, usage of this book.

ACKNOWLEDGEMENTS

I would like to take this opportunity to thank all the people who have witnessed my own various failures along the way. From childhood playmates, school-friends, school acquaintances, and school enemies; onward to work colleagues, bosses, potential bosses, and bosses without potential; finishing with random people who cannot explain why or how their lives should interact with mine: you have each been a chisel tap in the roughly hewn rock which has become the sculpture that is me. And it's still not finished. Okay, so it's no Michaelangelo, but it might be close enough for a Henry Moore.

Particular thanks go to those who still speak to me on a regular basis in spite of, or perhaps even because of, my failings. You know who you are. The God of your choice will reward you with chocolate biscuits, a nice cup of tea, and a bit of a sit-down in heaven.

And as for those of you who still don't speak to me on a regular basis: please consider the words of a man far wiser than myself. Sometimes the only purpose of a life is to serve as a warning to others. Let that be a lesson to you.

In the making of this book, I should like to thank all at New Holland – particularly Clare and Rosemary, my editors, for showing me how I ought to have written it.

Finally, thanks go to those people whose own failures have been represented within the pages of this book. The names have been hidden to protect the guilty.

CONTENTS

INTRODUCTION

If at first you don't succeed, failure may be your style.
Quentin Crisp

Let's face it. You are going to fail. There are few things more certain in life. Like death, taxes and bad driving, you can rely upon failure. Quite frankly, sometimes your best is just not good enough. For every winner, there must inevitably be a host of people who were pipped to the post. The law of averages alone would suggest that one of them is going to be you, at least once in your life. This is the sad but certain truth that we must all learn. But is it such a sad truth after all?

It is strange that we all seem to have such difficulty accepting this simple fact. Every day, this integral part of life is looked upon with shame and sadness, with feelings of embarrassment and inadequacy, with several bottles of scotch and with crying on stairs. Instead, what we ought to be doing is embracing our failure, taking it out to dinner, getting it drunk and making inept and uncoordinated attempts to have sex with it. Failure is neither good nor bad, it simply exists, and we must prepare ourselves to accept it. Only then can we explore our fullest potential to fail, and so achieve the greatest part of our humanity. This book teaches you how to come to terms with yourself as the miserable failure that you undoubtedly are, and how to enjoy yourself because of, rather than in spite of, your shortcomings and misdeeds. Across the full gamut of endeavour, we will seek out failure in an attempt to learn from it, understand it, laugh at it, and accept it as a fundamental part of human nature. To err, as the saying goes, is human.

Only once we have learnt to accept the inevitability of our own failure can we then get anything productive out of it. One of the first steps on the road to appreciating our failure in a new light is looking at how we view the failure of others. We all love to indulge in what the Germans call schadenfreude, which roughly translates as "shameful joy". Or, as Groucho Marx rather more succinctly put it, no one is completely unhappy at the failure of his best friend.

Comedy is, as the saying goes, tragedy plus distance. Other people's misfortunes have been a source of amusement ever since Og the caveman invented fire, and then accidentally burnt the fur coat he was wearing at the time. And so it goes on. The importance of this perspective should not be underrated, because it brings us to the rather unequal conclusion that someone else's failure is very funny, but our own is not: instead, it is a matter of great emotional concern and distress. There is something about this concept that is both paradoxical and deeply unfair. So, to better ourselves, we can either suggest that we should view everyone's failure with the same degree of angst, misery, frustration and despair as our own; or we can suggest that we should laugh out loud at our own risible performance, as we do for everyone else's. This latter approach has a number of advantages over the former. Firstly, it will fill the world with more mirth and happiness; secondly, it is based on a more realistic assessment of human nature. It is far easier to laugh at your own misfortune than it is to feel the same misery for the failings of others as for those of your own. Therefore, the key to coming to terms with your failure is to try to see it as others see it, and to appreciate the humour therein.

So, when you next fail at something, do not despair. Simply enjoy the ridiculousness, acknowledge the irony, and appreciate the attempt. As the old adage has it: laugh, and the world laughs with you. Cry, and you sleep alone.

Failure: Know Your Enemy

Aspiration

The fundamental cause of failure is aspiration. As soon as you start wanting to achieve things, you are in danger of failing in your attempt to acquire them. Aspiration comes in all shapes and sizes: it could be the house next door or the girl next door that tickles your fancy; you might wish to cross the Serengeti or just cross the road. As soon as you attempt to obtain your goal, you lay yourself wide open to the prospect of failure. If you never have a particular desire for a given outcome, then you will never be a failure. Consequently, only the truly indifferent man can live a life that is free from failure. However, there are very few of us who attain such a nirvana, and so we must all prepare to fail.

There are two main ways of failing: failure by error; and failure by omission. You can either do the wrong thing, or you can do nothing at all. The difficulty of making this choice lies in the fact that, sometimes, the correct course of action can only ever be determined after the event. This realisation is known as hindsight, a marvellous gift whereby we can say "I told you so", even if we didn't. There comes a point in everyone's life where you say to yourself, "if only I had remembered to turn the gas off", or "if only I hadn't lit that cigarette".

But hindsight, like irony, is a fickle mistress. Sometimes you might not know if you have failed for years after the event. On the other hand, you may discover, on your deathbed, that the one big failure which has blighted your life for decades was actually the correct thing to do after all. Thus, hindsight is a deeply subjective device, and not to be trusted. It is therefore impossible to assess failure in anything other than a subjective light. So you can never, truly, be sure that you have actually failed.

Embarrassment

Failure and embarrassment go hand in hand, like an old married couple. But embarrassment is, as a wise man once said, in the eye of the beholder. Shouting obscenities into the microphone at a karaoke bar may seem, at the time, the course of action of which you would be the most proud; and yet the next morning, you recoil with terror as the memory pushes its way to the front of your thoughts. We can be embarrassed by both words and actions that are inappropriate, which in hindsight may have not been the most sensible thing to have done. How many of us have found ourselves saying to ourselves "there is no way that this is not the right thing to do", only to find that everyone else is deeply shocked, upset, unamused or irritated by that very same act?

One particular element of embarrassment is the Comedy Displacement Error, or CDE. This is the mistaken belief that a particular joke, comment, action or set of vocabulary will be found highly amusing by one group of people at a given time and place, because it has previously been found highly amusing by a different group of people at a different time and place. Something that you might say to the lads down the pub might not be suitable material to use at a funeral, for example. Or, behaviour that your closest friends might tolerate, or even appreciate, may not receive the same consideration on your first day in a new job.

Another form of embarrassment is embarrassment by proxy. This is the feeling you get when, say, your dad attempts to dance, or when your grandmother tells highly explicit tales of her sexual adventures as a young girl – in fact whenever your relatives interact with you and your friends and acquaintances. This feeling is a mixture of empathic embarrassment on their behalf and a genuine, personal embarrassment for the fact that there is a very high genetic similarity between you and them. There are three things that you should bear in mind when you experience embarrassment by proxy. Firstly, it's not you. Secondly, it really isn't you this time. Thirdly, by the time you will be causing exactly the same level of grief to future generations, you won't notice either.

Embarrassment, like hindsight, is a highly subjective emotion. It depends upon the mood, the environment, the company and the weather. Consequently, it cannot be relied upon as any absolute yardstick by which we should measure ourselves, and it should be ignored and treated with the contempt and disdain it deserves. You must therefore feel no embarrassment at your failures. What you must do is treat them as others treat your failures: as a source of laughter and an amusing, if cautionary, tale to be told.

Don't Depress to Impress

Some people find that the continual catalogue of dismal failures that they have come to call a life can have a slightly depressing effect. Indeed, even laboratory rats have been shown to exhibit depression and pessimism at the state of their existence. But then, in fairness to lab rats everywhere, the existence of a lab rat is understandably quite depressing. You spend your whole life running around mazes or pressing levers, with no hope of remission until either animal rights activists or death bring you sweet release. On top of that, all the other rats will make fun of you, just because you've got a human ear growing out of your back.

Depression and Pessimism are both products of an unrealistic assessment of the world. However, depression is more egocentric, because it's all about you. Your life is rubbish, and everyone else's is much better. Pessimism, on the other hand, is usually more cynical and world-weary, with fewer suicidal tendencies. Pessimism, which might possibly be described as "a willingness for the Universe to underachieve", is actually a perverse longing for a worse result than you would actually like. Confusingly, this actually means that reality is much better than you expect, so a true pessimist should always be pleasantly surprised.

Self-pity, as my grandmother used to say, never peeled a potato. Whenever the black dog or brown study of depression rears its head, you must realise that it is a fundamentally fruitless exercise in navel-gazing. How much better to laugh at your misfortune, and to accept failure as an inevitable part of existence that you must learn from and then put aside? If nothing else, your failure will produce an amusing story that you can tell to your friends, if you have them, in the pub. Viewed in this way, even the most failed man in the world ought still to be a success by having no end of witty anecdotes. And the world will always need more witty anecdotes to tell in pubs.

Failure is therefore essential, if only as a means of getting people to buy you drinks.

The Consequences of Failure

Of course, failure does come with consequences, and it can sometimes be hard to see the laughter for the trees. You may have just bet your spouse on a hand in poker, or failed to earn the money that will keep the wolf, or rather the bailiffs, from the door. You may simply need to apologise to someone whose own view of failure and the use of violence is not as enlightened as your own. But you must remember that the further you fall, the funnier it is. All humour relies on this premise. These consequences only serve to distract us from the true lesson of failure, which is simply an opportunity to laugh at our own folly.

Failure Overseas

Failure, as we have seen, does not take place within a vacuum. Any failure on your part can easily be compounded, simply by performing it in a country whose culture or language you are unfamiliar with. If you encounter any local difficulties when travelling abroad, you might consider it useful to learn the local words for the following sentences before learning anything else:

- I am joking, of course; it was not my intention to offend.

- I have the highest respect for your mother.

- In my country, that is meant as a compliment.

- There appears to have been some sort of cultural misunderstanding.

- I apologise for my personal misjudgement.

- I would be more than happy to reimburse you.

Given that the chances of failure are so much higher in unfamiliar surroundings, it is beyond me why these essential phrases are absent from nearly every tourist guide and phrasebook, which, instead, simply instruct you how to buy cheese, or complain about a lack of soap in your hotel room.

The Wisdom of Failure

Strangely, in over five thousand years of recorded civilisation, I am not the first person to have spoken on the subject of failure. From the earliest times, man has recorded and celebrated his successes, writ large in hieroglyphs and declared with monoliths. However, there has also been a subversive undercurrent, occasionally revealing that the Ancients, for all their arcane wisdom, were just as capable of making monumental cock-ups as they were of making monuments. All of this goes to show that while civilisations and technologies comes and go, human error remains constant through the millennia. There is the old adage, "if at first you don't succeed, try, try, try again". Note that the word "try" is used three times. If you can't do it after three goes, you should probably give up. No-one likes a stubborn man who doesn't know his own limitations.

It was Friedrich Nietzsche who famously said that what does not kill us makes us stronger. Of course, he was riddled with syphilis at the time, so it's best to take this advice with a pinch of salt. Or, at the very least, a regular course of penicillin.

There is also, apparently, an old adage which has it that "three failures and a fire make a Scotsman wealthy". Unless the Scotsman in question has exceptionally good insurance cover, I can't really see how this arrangement would work. But it may well come in handy to know this at some point in your life.

The Chinese, who have been purveyors of esoteric wisdom for millennia, tell us that the great question of life is not whether you have failed, but whether you are content with failure. Like a lot of Taoist philosophy, it loses a little in translation and can appear ambiguous. It is perhaps unclear here whether you should strive to improve yourself, or rather just sit back with a nice cup of tea. This author favours and recommends the latter approach as the wiser course of action. You should therefore be content with your own failure, as something that defines you as much as your success.

The rest of the this book is divided into sections detailing various fields of failure, arenas of personal shortcomings and spheres of ineptitude. The lessons have been garnered from individual experience, anecdotal evidence and pending legal cases. When you next consider your own failures, it is hoped that the instances, examples and universals contained in this book will bring some comfort to you, by showing that we are all – even the greatest among us – miserable failures. In other words: no, it's not just you.

Once you have learnt this, it is only a small step to see the humour in your own misdeeds, for it is laughter that reconciles us to our frailties.

CHAPTER 1
INTERVIEWS

Success and failure are equally disastrous.
Tennessee Williams

Before you begin to fail within the confines of your chosen career, you must actually have a career. For most of us, acquiring employment means attending some form of interview, which is the perfect opportunity both to fail and to show off your failings and inadequacies.

Back in the old days, candidates for jobs were selected on the basis of their parentage and education. And so it was that someone with one surname would automatically be selected over another, one university preferred over another, and one school favoured in much the same way, all according to the personal preference of the interview panel. Whilst this was remarkably unfair, it was at least consistent, and you could tell who would get the job without actually having to go to the trouble of interviewing all the candidates. Nowadays, people are, rather irritatingly, assessed on their merits, which are an elusive and well-hidden bunch of attributes at the best of times. It is not entirely clear exactly who came up with the idea that people's merits could be assessed through the medium of an interview – perhaps because it is not the sort of idea for which people might want to take credit. Also, given that senior managers must spend weeks interviewing several candidates, who themselves have to take time off work in order to attend, more man-hours are lost to the nation from interviews than from illness, slacking, or surfing the net for pornography.

The interview is a tried and tested business tool for selecting personnel according to merit. The process goes something like this: An advertisement is placed in a newspaper by the company, to which around one hundred people might reply. Of these, a handful is selected to attend an interview. This group is whittled down to two or three, who are called back for a second interview. Finally, the office junior, who has been doing the work whilst the position was vacant, is appointed and all the interviewees are rejected.

> *You may not even have to fail*
> *the interview, as you can*
> *be pre-failed beforehand.*

Thanks, but No Thanks

Having applied for a position, there is of course no guarantee that you will actually make it to the interview stage. You may be spared the embarrassment of appearing in person at all. You may not even have to fail the interview, as you can be pre-failed beforehand. There are many different ways in which companies will break the news to you. The five most common are:

The Silent
The company does not acknowledge your application or indeed your very existence. If you telephone them, you will only speak to people who know nothing about recruitment or indeed anything else.

The Phase 1
You receive a prompt letter, thanking you for applying. They inform you that they are now considering all the applications, and that you will be rejected on a given date in the future.

The Pre-emptive
This is where small print in the original job advertisement tells you that everyone will fail in their application unless they hear to the contrary.

The Sympathetic
You receive a seemingly personal letter, in the style of an apology, stating that you are "overqualified for the role". What they mean is, of course, that you asked for too high a salary.

The Judicial
You are served with a restraining order, which forbids you from contacting anyone at the company, or being within 100 feet of their premises.

A Test of Character
Once you have actually been asked to attend the interview, you must then carefully decide how to present the particular blend of

characteristics that you have come to call "your personality". An established city law firm is unlikely to be looking for an unpredictable maverick who works alone and plays outside the system; conversely, a creative advertising agency may not be interested in funny handshakes and old school ties.

Of course, there is more than one way to skin a cat. (And if you've ever failed trying that, my advice is to get the scratches disinfected as soon as possible.) Here are a few archetypal methods of behaving at interview and of coping with the inevitable rejection that follows them. They may not guarantee failure, and they are not necessarily recommended tactics; but, should you find yourself adopting one of these traditional techniques, you can at least take comfort from the fact that you are not the first to have walked the path.

The Confident
You are the best candidate for the job, and you're going to tell them so. Your underwear is more expensive that the entire wardrobe of the interview panel. Quite frankly, only an imbecile would consider anyone else for the job.

You react with apoplexy to your rejection and write a letter to *The Times* in protest. Make sure to say "never seen anything quite so unprofessional in my whole life".

The Clown
You like to think your personality makes up for any holes in your CV,

but in fact, it's responsible for most of them – particularly that "year out" in a Turkish prison. You respond to serious questions about your abilities with cheap gags and sexual innuendo.

You laugh when you learn of your rejection, joking about it with all your friends. Like all clowns, you secretly cry yourself to sleep.

The Indifferent

Frankly, you don't care whether you get the job or not. You're only going to interviews to annoy your current employer, anyway.

You react to your rejection in much the same way that you react when your grandmother tells you she went to the shops yesterday.

The Desperate

You don't want this job. You need it. You have dreamt of it since you were a small child, and you tell the interviewer that it is the fulfilment of your destiny. You tell him again, in case he didn't hear you properly.

You weep as you read the rejection letter, cursing the world and drinking deep from the well of bitterness.

The Mumbler

You slouch in your chair, with your head angled to one side. Your answers are monosyllabic and possibly augmented by a shrug of the shoulders. You choose to be withdrawn and uncommunicative. When asked to explain your actions, you reply "Dunno", without ever making eye contact with the panel.

Your reaction to your rejection is indistinct.

The Drunk

You kill time before your interview by going to the pub. You may choose to take some pills a friend gave you "to help calm your nerves". You arrive late, smelling like a distillery. A distillery that smokes 40 a day. Your answers are incoherent and abusive. You tell the interview panel that you love them, and then start a fight with one of them.

You react with surprise to the rejection, as you can't remember attending the interview.

Stupid Questions: Stupid Answers

In your quest for failure, you are not alone. As luck would have it, interviewers specialise in providing fatuous and risible questions, which enable you to provide answers of equal risibility and fatuousness. They are kindly offering you the opportunity to display levels of crassness and stupidity which are guaranteed to fail.

So, tell me about yourself.

This is a classic. It gives the pretence of interest, without actually having to ask a specific question relevant to the candidate. In your reply, it is important to include some information that is either absent from, or contradictory to, your CV. This will keep your interviewer on his toes.

"It was my involvement with the CIA in South America that first got me interested in logistics."

"I try not dwell on my life before the nervous breakdown."

Describe yourself in three words.

In the guise of a serious psycho-analytical tool, this question is a mere parlour game. If your name comprises three words, simply state your name, telling them that this is how you are described, and you've got the paperwork to prove it. Alternatively, use the numerical limitation to your advantage.

"Competent, and yet..."

What are your weaknesses?

This is, quite literally, asking for trouble. No-one in their right mind is actually going to tell the interviewer of any major failings they may have, like an inability to read, or a pathological dislike of other people. You therefore find yourself trying to make up something that probably won't seem applicable to the daily grind of work.

"I have a weakness for cheese."

"I always tell my plans for world domination to secret agents I have captured."

If you were an animal, what type of animal would you be, and why?

Again, a rather surreal question posing as some sort of psycho-analytical tool. Its bizarreness may leave you feeling like a rabbit caught in headlights, so that would be a good answer for starters. Choose any animal (extra points for obscure or rare creatures) and a characteristic that is unlikely to be of use within the field of your employment.

"A guinea-pig. They eat their young."

"A Patagonian throaty reed warbler. The male keeps a coterie of up to six wives."

How would your friends describe you?

This is superb nonsense. Your perception of your friends' perception of yourself is not really an index of either your character or your business proficiency. Treat this with the contempt it deserves:

"I have no friends that I am aware of."

"I only have one friend, and he thinks I'm a complete bastard."

Hobbies

In the unlikely event of two or more candidates being equally suitable for a position, an employer will often look at the candidates' personal interests as a means of separating the wheat from the chaff. It is sometimes thought that well-rounded candidates should indulge in a great many extracurricular activities, to show that they can take the demands of the job in their stride and still have time to do other things. However, as we all know, hobbies are the domain of obsessive compulsive types. No normal people have hobbies. And yet we feel obliged to "invent" a range of interests and activities, placing them on our CV to make us seem more interesting than we might otherwise be. Despite this, there is no activity or pastime that cannot and will not be looked upon with sinister overtones or some degree of suspicion. Placing any hobby, real or invented, on a CV merely offers the interviewer another opportunity to find fault and fail you.

What we say

I'm interested in French Art Cinema.

I'm in the Campaign for Real Ale.

I spend a lot of time reading.

I go to the gym regularly.

I enjoy Amateur Dramatics.

I'm in the Territorial Army.

I like classic car restoration.

I'm an amateur photographer.

I'm a member of a local club/society.

I'm a member of the Pony Club.

I'm a Scout Master.

What they think we mean

I have an extensive pornographic video collection.

I'm a serious alcoholic.

I think a basic skill is something to be proud of.

I try to pick up people in the jacuzzi.

I'm a cross-dresser.

I'm a gun-crazy loner.

My car is one step away from being a death trap.

I'm a Peeping Tom.

I'm a swinger.

I'm an upper class swinger.

I'm a Scout Master.

Needless to say, the interview panel will always chose the most unwholesome interpretation of anything you might suggest (see pages 26–27). Your only hope of success is if the interviewer holds the same interests as you profess to. If you are unfortunate enough to get the job, you will then have to spend time outside work with your boss, developing an unhealthy interest in pottery, car boot sales, or naked rambling.

Salary Negotiations

If you have managed to avoid failure right up to the point of being offered the job, there then comes the awkward discussion of money. Here, failure is not so much black-and-white, but rather comes in shades of grey. The reason salary negotiations are so feared and fraught is that they place a numerical value upon your worth. This makes it very easy to decide who is more important than whom, and also the likely reaction of your employer when you threaten to walk out if you don't get your way. Many men have found out the answer to "Either he goes, or I go" the hard way.

But it is surely a strange thing to ask someone to put a value upon themselves. Choose a number that is too high, and you will be seen as arrogant, misguided, and unrealistic. Choose a number that is too low, and you will be doing yourself a disservice. Some salary negotiations can resemble games of bluff, like poker, with each side unwilling to show their hand until they can put something on the table and win. And as with all games of chance and bluff, there are no sure-fire rules, and all bets are off. *Rien ne va plus, les jeux sont fait,* as they say in France.

Useful techniques in salary negotiations include saying any or all of the following:

- "A gentleman never discusses tawdry finance."

- "I'll trust you to give me what's fair."

- "I think I bring a higher level of value than the market place would suggest."

- "I'll have whatever you're having."

Auditions

Those in the performing arts – actors, musicians, magicians and clowns – have to attend auditions rather than interviews to secure work. The essential difference between an audition and an interview is that an audition is an actual test of the skills for which you are being hired, whereas an interview is not. Also, if someone calls you "darling" in an audition, you would probably be quite pleased; whereas you would find it slightly worrying in an interview. Consequently, there are only two reasons why you might not be selected for the gig. Either someone else really was more suited to the role than you, or you're just not sleeping with the right people. Which of these is the case may take many years of trial and error to establish.

Final Thoughts

It's often said that a useful technique for overcoming nerves at interview is to imagine the interviewer naked. This is strange psychosexual advice for what is, after all, merely a conversation. From personal experience, I can confidently say that pointing and staring in wide-eyed disbelief at someone's crotch during an interview enhances one's suitability for very few jobs. And when it does work, it's probably not going to be within your ideal career path.

Chapter 2
Business

*One must be a god to be able to tell success from
failure without making a mistake.*
Anton Chekhov

Business is, more than any other field of endeavour, the area where
failure would seem to be least well-received. This may be because
failure in business can have much more wide-reaching consequences,
such as people losing money, and their jobs, and their houses. And
their family and friends. And their sense of self-worth. And their
dignity. For the most part, people tend to take these things quite
seriously, and it can be difficult for some to appreciate the humour in
the achievements of a lifetime, shattered like shards of pottery on a
marble floor. This is particularly true when the failure is not even a
result of your own incompetence, but simply caused by the vagaries
of the marketplace.

Despite the often high stakes, failure still occurs in business as
much as anywhere else. The world of business would doubtless like to
portray itself as a world of winners, of slick salesmen clinching deals
and meeting targets, punching the sky and whooping in cheap
suits. That is what we are led to believe. As we have already learnt, any

competition will have at least one loser – and business is nothing if not competitive.

Those of you with a penchant for failing in business should get yourself a seat on the board as soon as possible.

Somewhat perversely, it is possible in this high-pressure environment to be rewarded for failure. Whilst some workers will be instantly dismissed without further remuneration for petty breaches of regulations, company directors are often showered with gifts, even when they have been shown to be utterly hopeless. Profits may be down, sales at rock bottom, but if you are forced off the board, you still take a big stack of cash and shares with you. Of course, the shares may not be worth as much as they were when you started, but it's still more than the machine operator gets, when he is sacked for leaving that safety catch off. Consequently, those of you with a penchant for failing in business should get yourself a seat on the board as soon as possible – and there is some evidence that this does indeed happen.

Business and commerce are clearly no strangers to blunder, and sometimes they even promote and encourage it. Not for nothing is the popular expression "errors and omissions excepted", or E&OE, appended to most business contracts. This device enables you to crawl away from your obligations in any contract you have signed where the decimal point is in the wrong place, or the word "not" is omitted from several key sentences.

But is it any wonder that the world of business engenders so much failure when it creates its own language? For some inexplicable reason, it is common commercial practice to abstract language into uselessness. It is almost as if there is a competition to see who can use the word, phrase or sentence that means the least. When no-one knows what anyone else is talking about, panic and error cannot be far away. If you hear any of the following phrases, it is safe to assume that one of you does not understand what is being said, and the other probably does not understand what he or she is saying.

- I want to see an 80% performance quantum leap.

- Let's run it up the flagpole and see who jumps into bed with it.

- To provide added value best practice quality management, we are undergoing a sector paradigm shift that will inevitably lead to down-sizing.

Things to Say at Work

Commerce, of course, promotes a competitive atmosphere. And the one thing we have learnt so far in our exploration of failure is that competition leads to failure. The best way to irritate and infuriate the go-getters and sharp-shooters within your place of work is not to play the game, by displaying a complete lack of interest in all things relating to money. Here are some examples:

- "Never mind. It's only money."

- "It's not that important in the cosmic order of things."

- "In a hundred years, who'll care?"

- "If it was only about making money, we wouldn't be in this business sector."

- "Woah. That's just such bad karma."

The Presentation

At your place of work, you will inevitably be required to give a presentation to potential customers, team members, shareholders or other people. The most important thing to remember is that no-one wants to be listening to you right now. They would much rather be talking about golf at the bar.

In order to hold their interest, a whole industry has grown up around the business presentation, providing you with slide projectors, computer software, overhead video and has-been celebrities. Whilst these are traditionally considered to be the hallmarks of a failed public speaker, you must remember that they actually serve to distract your audience from the mediocrity of the information you are relaying and your risible performance as a speaker. In order to hide your dim light under a burning bushel, you must do all or some of the following.

- Display the words you are saying onto the wall behind you. If you can make them flash, so much the better.

- Show a twenty-minute film that could be more usefully summarised in one sentence.

- Use slides to illustrate even the most basic concept.

- Hire some disco lights and a glitter ball. And some dancers.

- Use a sound system that might once have been quite good in the 1970s.

- Always remember that your choice of computer graphics should be extremely patronising to your audience, who obviously cannot read anything unless it is displayed in very large 3D type.

- Use a stick (or a light pointer for maximum effect) to point at items in your presentation – the more painfully obvious, the better. Say the words "here, here, and especially here" as you point.

- Finally, if you can manage it, book some ageing sports star (preferably one who has disgraced himself in some way or succumbed to the temptations of drugs and alcohol), to persuade your audience that meeting corporate targets involves the same physical agility and co-ordination as that of an athlete.

There is a little known fundamental law of nature, known to only a handful of physicists and philosophers, that governs the use of slide projectors or digital image carousels in any presentation. Intricate mathematical equations and the hand of God conspire against you, so that strange, unnatural events now become certainties. No matter how hard you prepare, no matter what steps you take to prevent it, at least one of the following things will happen.

- You will get one slide out of order.

- Another will be upside down or the wrong way round.

- You will accidentally include a photo of you on holiday, usually drunk and wearing very little, and be forced to say to your audience "I don't know how that got there".

Do not worry. This cannot be considered a failure, as it is impossible to avoid. You must resign yourself to your fate and simply accept the cosmic inevitability of the situation, and move on. Next slide please.

The history of the world teaches us nothing except that people generally do not get on well together, particularly when one is put in a position of authority over others.

People Management

As with any interaction between people, the management of staff is yet another area where we can fail. One of the first mistakes made is to refer to "human resources", when in fact you mean "people", as the former makes your employees feel about as significant as any other company asset, such as paper clips, pencils or post-it notes.

In your dealings with those for whom you are responsible, you can adopt a range of attitudes, techniques and ploys in order to successfully manage your team. You are, however, going to fail whatever you do, as the history of the world teaches us nothing except that people generally do not get on well together, particularly when one is put in a position of authority over others. You may scream and shout, cry, belittle, bully, berate, toy, joke or run away hiding. You may even – and worst of all – attempt to be reasonable with your charges. The prospect of a reasonable boss fills most workers with terror, because it means that they cannot blame decisions against their favour on their boss's glaringly obvious sociopathic problems, but have to come to the conclusion that, in fairness, he probably does have a point after all.

Some people try to avoid conflict with their colleagues by avoiding them, hiding on the lavatory for the entire working day if necessary. Others choose to actively seek out conflict with those around them, breaking down the toilet door if they must. Neither strategy is either constructive or guaranteed to be successful.

Of course, your own failures and those of your colleagues will interact with each other. Your boss's failures make you look good, particularly if you are not making those mistakes yourself and can show him up in front of his boss. The errors of your subordinates will reflect poorly on you, as you are at least nominally responsible for their actions. The failure of your peers can be looked upon as with kindness and sympathy, and you should help them to correct or hide them, as necessary. As for your own errors, they are of course just idiosyncratic character flaws, for which you are rightly loved by one and all.

Competence?

One often quoted theory of people management is the Peter Principle, which is the concept that an individual will continue to be promoted for success until he stops succeeding. At that point, he has been promoted into a job beyond his level of competence. This means that everyone is becoming less competent as they move up the career ladder at work. Studies show that 10% of the working population is incompetent, although this may seem like a lower figure than a quick glance around your office might suggest. Combined with the Peter Principle, it can be clearly demonstrated that the office tea-boy is the only competent member of your staff with adequate training for his role. He can make tea better than anyone else can file, manage, operate, assess, control, analyse, account, or direct. The rest of your organisation is increasingly incompetent and inefficient. Therefore, to maximise the efficiency and competence of any business, you should sell all your assets and open a small tea shop. However, if every company in the world started running tea-shops, some of them would, no doubt, be better than others, and inevitably one of them would have the least qualified tea-makers.

The Public Sector

Those who have sensibly found the cut and thrust of corporate life too demanding for their meagre talents and aspirations, but who still need to be gainfully employed, have an alternative area of business open to them. This is a very well-practised business model where failure is nurtured, and is known as the public sector. This comprises organisations that appear business-like, but are not actually businesses, such as governments, museums, charities, schools and such like. The major difference between these organisations and conventional businesses is that they are neither required to make money, nor to be efficient in the spending of their money, nor indeed to do the job properly. If a government department has a budget given to it, it knows that it must spend all of that money – and perhaps some more as well. What it does with the money is pretty much irrelevant, as long as it is seen to be spending it. The same can be said of schools, hospitals and charities. Consequently, it is very difficult to establish any criterion for failure within such organisations, and so it is that many people, who might otherwise fail in a more demanding environment, can make a career for themselves – or at least hide quietly in an office until they retire. The public sector is called by its name because it provides a remarkable public service, occupying people who are just not cut out for achieving any particular goals and who tend towards failure. This fact is rarely appreciated by private sector businesses, who ought to do more to help the public sector keep people in employment who might otherwise fail in the private sector.

Business Reorganisation

Periodically, businesses tire of their habitual failures, and make a futile attempt to re-invigorate the company. One commonly used method of disguising commercial failure is by announcing what is known as "a major internal restructuring". This is an attempt to separate the people who are failing within an organisation from those people who know who the failures are. This would seem to be the perfect moment to cut out the dead wood and unproductive elements of the business, but what tends to happen is that the dead wood is simply hidden deep within the more profitable sections of the organisation. In this way, the failure is smoothed out, and its effect minimised – or so the theory has it. The actual effect is to confuse everybody, nurturing and encouraging more failure that before. To show that business reorganisation is nothing new, here is an extract from the diary of Petronius Arbitor, the Roman Governor of Bythnia in the 1st century AD.

> "We trained hard, but it seemed that every time we were beginning to form up in teams, we would be reorganised. I was to learn later in life that we tend to meet any new situation by reorganising, and a wonderful method it can be for creating the illusion of progress, whilst producing confusion, inefficiency and demoralisation".

Sadly, he committed suicide in AD 65, as the result of one reorganisation too many. It would appear that business management techniques have not really improved in the last two thousand years or so.

Meetings

The purpose of meetings is to avoid blame for decisions by blaming the meeting or the committee itself: both of them are abstract concepts and neither of them is you. That is, of course, provided you actually get as far as making a decision in a meeting. Meetings offer a great many things: a cup of tea, biscuits, the chance of a nap and failure, in equal measure. Unfortunately, here you might be called upon to supply factually accurate information on which others may rely. You could even be asked to explain what you have been doing these last few weeks – and "surfing the Internet" probably won't suffice as an answer. Worst of all, you may even be asked to give your opinion. The prospect for failure, in front of your peers and superiors, could not be greater.

Meetings are traditionally held in rooms where the air circulation is totally inadequate for the number of people in attendance, which leads to increasing levels of carbon dioxide. It is for this reason that lethargy, yawning, and even sleep are prevalent in meetings. If someone does start to snore whilst you are speaking, you should take comfort that they have not fallen asleep because of your metaphorical hot air, but rather physical hot air. Conversely, if you yourself succumb to dreaming, you have a scientifically verifiable excuse for doing so. But, as with operating heavy machinery, attending a meeting when tired can make you more prone to error.

A useful thing to say in a meeting, in response to someone who is confident of their facts and not playing the failure game, is to reply "I'm not sure if that is actually the case". If said in the right way, it can sound as if you are rebuking the validity of the facts being presented. If it later becomes patently clear that the facts are true, you can simply dismiss your comment as an indication that you just weren't sure. Meetings are also the scene of many public humiliations, where you can be shown up in front of everyone else. When asked a question to which you don't have the answer at hand, a useful tip is to lower your head in shame and say in a near whisper, "Don't know, sir. Sorry, sir." For greatest effect, you can giggle and nudge the person sitting next to you.

Courses & Seminars

Courses and Seminars, particularly those held away at hotels or conference centres, are noted for two things. Firstly, the summary of knowledge acquired could have been more profitably learnt in one hour spent with a slim book than in one week's all-inclusive junket. Secondly, you could cut the sexual tension in the air with a knife. The prospect of a couple of nights away from home in the anonymous surroundings of a cheap hotel work their magic and failure beckons with its inevitable lure as neither the thirst for knowledge nor the hunger of lust are sated. Everyone returns to their offices and spouses, confident that the exercise was a valuable use of company funds. No-one needs be any the wiser.

Final Thoughts

Occasionally, commerce generates a rare phenomenon of mass failure. This starts with an eager expectation of success, which grows so fast that the expectation cannot possibly be matched by reality. The South Sea Bubble, the Great Tulip Hype, and the Dotcom fiasco are all instances of collective failure through collective action. This is the marvellous event, when hundreds or thousands of people co-operate and work together to achieve a failure far greater than any one man could attempt by himself. The most mundane instance of group failure is known as a meeting, where decisions are reached by many people that no individual person would make on their own.

CHAPTER 3
ROMANCE

Success always occurs in private and failure in full public view.
Anon

Of course, it is on the ship of love that most of us first run aground upon the rocks of failure, drawn in by the lighthouse of hope. We can all tell tales of teenage crushes and youthful devotion from afar. We all know of the hesitant moment when we first revealed our tortured secret to the object of our affection, only to be ridiculed and laughed at by them and all our peers, because Sally Grainger told the whole school that break-time.

Everyone in the world falls in love with someone at some time in their life; and everyone in the world is also loved at some point. However, the two things do not necessarily always happen at the same time, nor to the same people, and it is here that failure enters the stage. Your romantic failure depends upon interaction with other people within an environment. Failure never occurs in isolation, even if it leads to it.

To fully appreciate the possibilities of romantic failure, you must first understand the way in which people interact with each other.

There is a complex system which governs how you react to people, and how people react to you. You might be a sculpted Adonis, a comely Venus, or just someone who buys the "meals for one" from the supermarket. To illustrate this point, I should like to draw a Venn diagram. Why? For two reasons. Firstly, it would seem to explain the point I want to make quite well; and secondly, because I have never seen a Venn diagram outside the Maths lesson in which I was taught them. I would therefore like to offer Maths teachers everywhere a real world example.

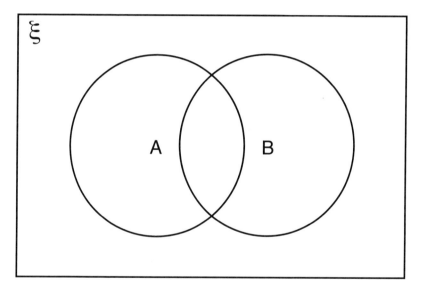

The Universal Set, ξ, represents all the people you know. Set A contains all the people to whom you might possibly be attracted. Set B contains all the people who might possible be attracted to you. And the intersection of the two circles contains those people to whom you might be attracted who might actually be attracted to you. The above diagram represents the state of affairs for most people; however, a range of different graphs can be produced, depending on the size of the intersection between the two sets.

At one extreme end of the scale, A could be a subset of B:

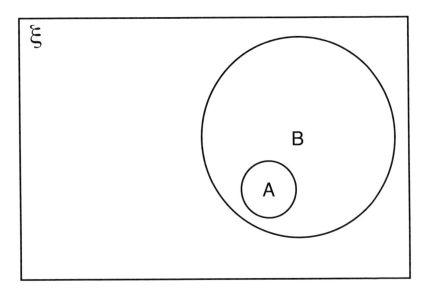

In this instance, you are blessed in that everyone you like feels the same way about you. The only disadvantage comes in the form of unwanted attention, from those in the rest of set B. You are obviously some sort of sex god.

At the other end of the scale lies a very different proposition. B could be a subset of A:

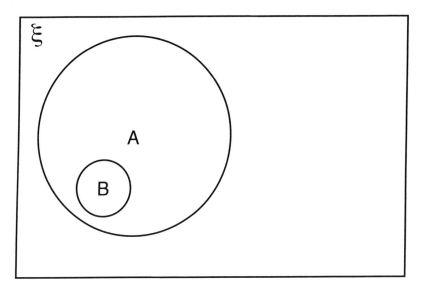

Here, you are willing to accept the advances of everyone who likes you, and your only problem is whether others will accept your own advances. That, and maintaining interest, given your fickle nature. You are, quite clearly, a tart.

Failure never occurs in isolation, even if it leads to it.

In the worst-case scenario, the intersection could even be an empty set.

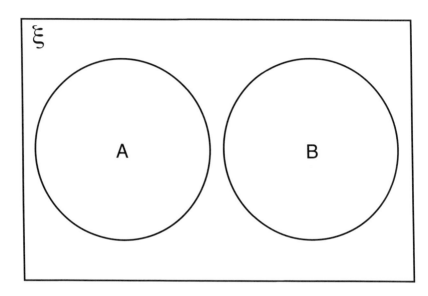

In this case, you must immediately do at least one of the following. Meet more people, undergo some sort of fundamental image change, or drastically lower your standards.

Those in the Universal set who are neither in set A nor B are, for the most part, your friends – or at least those of them with whom you have agreed that you are never, ever going to sleep together.

On the strength of these diagrams, it's a wonder that the human population survives at all. But contrary to the apparent difficulty of the whole exercise, we have the frightening statistic that, at any given moment, approximately 100 million people are having sex. Now that's the kind of party I never get invited to. And, I would suggest that in order to achieve that statistic, some people must have been putting in a double shift.

Places to Meet Your Future Ex

There are a number of places where you are likely to fail in your attempts to meet a future ex partner. These are all well-trodden paths where generations before you have, miraculously, managed to produce subsequent generations, in spite of all the problems that stood in their way. While people come and go, the problems remain, and they are listed here so that you can experience and recognise them for yourself.

Disco 2000

It is perhaps a little bizarre that the place where many people go to meet potential partners is a large, dark room, with music so loud that conversation is all but impossible. In order to further disorientate you and impair your judgment, coloured lights are flashed into your face, and you've been drinking. Failure here is therefore easily achieved. In this environment, it's imperative to keep any conversation short and banal. The following sentences can only be met with failure and rejection in a disco:

- "I've always liked the unusual harmonic progression in that song."

- "What do you think about the Aristotelian dichotomy of form and function?"

- "Do you think Post-modernism encourages artists to be lazy?"

It is only at the end of the evening – and by "evening" I obviously mean 4 or 5 in the morning – that the music stops playing and the house lights go on. Only then might there be the possibility of normal conversation and a reasonable assessment of someone's physical attributes. Of course, you can't hear because your ears are still ringing, and you still can't actually see or talk properly, because you've been drinking for a good six hours. Alternatively, you may have taken so many drugs that you would have sex with a table, if it gave you the slightest encouragement. The little tease.

The Dinner Party

If you are a single person who has a number of friends that are either married or in long-term relationships, you may be unfortunate enough to be invited to a dinner party. After arriving and meeting the assembled throng, you will soon work out that you and one other person are the only single people there, and that the whole reason for the party is a concerned but misguided attempt to pair the two of you together. This immediately raises a few questions of etiquette. Are you under an obligation to make a pass, in order to be polite to your hosts? If the two of you do hit it off, would the dinner be a success or a failure if you started having sex on the table? Before dessert?

However, what tends to happen is that both of the single people realise what has been planned, and spend the entire evening grinning through their teeth and making false pleasantries. Neither wants to give the impression of being desperate or easy (though this may well be the case) and so a rather pointless stalemate is declared with neither side making any move. The hosts can't understand what went wrong, and so try to fix each of the singles with other single friends they know. The circle of failure revolves once more. (In any case, your married friends are not matchmaking out of any genuine concern for your happiness, but rather just because they want someone else to talk to about babies.)

Occasionally, a dinner party will occur where everyone is single. In this rare instance, everyone will talk about how much they enjoy being single, and how refreshing it is to go to a dinner party where there isn't any pressure from the host to chat someone up. This either makes any potential romantic encounter impossible, or the whole thing turns into one big orgy. The latter will usually occur only when the desserts have been made to resemble rude shapes. Of course, the orgy variety only exists in other people's lives, and never in your own.

The Workplace
Most people, it is claimed, meet their partners at work. And yet, people often advise their friends against office romances, and some companies even have regulations prohibiting them. The uncomfortable metaphor "crapping on your own doorstep" is used. (Although probably not in office regulations, admittedly.) Inevitably, you will spend a lot of time with the people you work with: year in, year out; eight hours a day, five days a week. This could be more time than you spend with your friends. Or indeed would wish to.

Of course, the majority of office lechery occurs, legendarily, at the Christmas party. It is here that, fuelled by large quantities of drink, the pent-up sexual frustration of the past twelve months is released with gay abandon. Sometimes, with abandon that is more gay than had previously been suspected. Like some kind of mediaeval Day of Misrule, this is also the time for secretaries to turn the tables by sexually harassing their bosses.

Traditionally, the stationery cupboard is the scene for much of the action at office parties. For my part, I can think of few places less suited to the job in hand. Anywhere where accidents with pencils might occur and the risk of paper-cuts is high does not lend itself to an entirely trouble-free union.

It's a little known fact that the photocopier was actually invented so that office workers at parties could position their bottoms on the glass plate without their underwear and distribute the pictures. Necessity is, after all, the mother of invention. The copying of office documents was an unexpected bonus that had not originally occurred to its inventors.

After the hedonistic excess of the office party has faded, there is often much embarrassment the following day, once you realise that you still have to maintain some kind of professional relationship with the person with whom you were performing acts that constitute public decency offences. This is usually where the events of the previous evening transcend into failure. Some try the tactic of denying the whole encounter. Some merely use the excuse of drunkenness as the ultimate mitigation. Some choose to never speak to that particular colleague ever again.

The House Party

A loose collection of friends and acquaintances, plied with drink and strange snacks, wandering around a house, would seem to be the best mechanism for social intercourse, if not other varieties. How could failure be made manifest here? Well, house parties involve the deft art of mingling, a seemingly simple activity that is in fact fraught with difficulty. The problem of mingling can be summed up thus. You have a limited time in which to talk to a finite number of people at the party. Using your skill and judgment (a risky proposition at the best of times), you must then decide how much of your time to divide between each person. You might talk all night to the first person you have been introduced to, not realising that your soul-mate is standing in the next room; or you might spread yourself too thinly, saying nothing more than "Hello" and "Where's the bathroom?" to each person in turn, so that you are hardly noticed by anyone. The middle ground between these two extremes is what usually tends to happen, whereby you get stuck talking to someone who bores you to tears.

The true, professional mingler will arrive when most people are already there, and will make one swift sweep of the entire party. He, or she, will then select the person they find most promising, and spend the rest of the evening getting to know them, confident in the knowledge that there is no-one more interesting that they have missed. The problem with this strategy, of course, is the Unforeseen. Guests arriving late, or leaving early; the need to go for food and drink; queuing for the toilet – all these things put the mingler's plan in jeopardy and promote failure.

The alternative to mingling is the LCF (Lowest Common Factor) technique. This is by far the most commonly used method at parties. For this, all you need to do is get very, very drunk. Anyone who is still talking to you has seen you at your worst and is still interested. Whilst this may deter any number of potential suitors, the technique can be quite successful. An astonishing 8% of all married couples first met their future spouses whilst one of them was vomiting into a lavatory bowl. Which is no mean feat in itself.

The Dinner Date

The most popular, tried and tested method of failing involves taking your potential partner to a restaurant. Restaurants contain a host of pratfalls and problems with which you can embarrass yourself. First of all is the food itself: you can send it flying to the next table while trying to cut it into pieces; then you can spill it down your front when bringing it to your mouth. Next is the patronising waiter: he will happily treat your foolhardy attempt to pronounce the name of your food with a French, Italian or other accent with the contempt it deserves. Your only opportunity to thwart him is to say "Hmm! I don't think he will be getting a tip", which just makes you look cheap in front of your date.

Finally, there are any number of health and safety hazards to look out for, such as naked flames, sharp cutlery, and table legs that have been carefully aligned with your kneecaps. Once you have negotiated your way around these obstacles, you then have to talk to your date, which is perhaps the most risky proposition of them all.

Flirting & Small Talk

An apparently straightforward attempt to strike up a conversation can become a minefield of despair and failure, particularly when you are trying to impress the other person. You will try to achieve the fine distinction of appearing confident without seeming arrogant; interested, but not disturbingly so; enigmatic, and yet open; keen, but not perverted. Exactly where the line should be drawn depends entirely upon the company. Inevitably, you will fold under the pressure, and find yourself saying that you were personally responsible for any number of war atrocities, simply because you were searching for some conversational gambit to break the interminable silence.

Even the seemingly simple task of flirting can be fraught with difficulty. It is not to be entered into lightly, but with great care and cunning. In some circumstances, flirting can actually be hazardous to one's health. It should never be attempted when crossing a busy road, for instance. Nor when the six-foot six boyfriend of your paramour is standing next to you. However, the more usual failures in the art of flirting are merely the product of ill-timing and ill-judgment. There are boundaries to the form that flirting can take. Rubbing yourself against the object of your affection is not likely to get you the result you are seeking. The usual response to unwelcome or inappropriate flirting is an expression of horror, profound distaste at the remarks, and a desperate clutching at a mobile phone in order to call the police.

Rejection

Rejection is romantic failure made manifest. There are two main forms of romantic rejection. There is rejection of an advance, and there is rejection of an existing relationship, otherwise known as "dumping". Rejection of an advance is the easier and quicker of the two, and can range from a simple but firm "No", through the witty "There's not enough beer in the world," to the more wistful "I'd rather stick pins in my eyes". A wide range of clichés and stock expressions are now available to those seeking to rid themselves of a potential suitor. The more hackneyed the rejection, the more obvious it is, leaving little opportunity for misunderstanding. As a consequence of this social custom, the sentence "I'm afraid I'm washing my hair tonight" is never used in its literal sense, without any subtext.

Most people accept rejection with good grace, slinking quietly back to their place, secretly vowing never to let this happen again. However, a recent trend is to rejoinder the rejection, hitting back with a winning retort to ease the awkwardness and dull the pain. For instance, in reply to the rejection "I don't want a relationship to spoil the friendship we have", a suitor might say "That's alright – I never liked you that much anyway."

The use of such a witty comeback to restore your shrunken pride and make you seem nonchalant, indifferent and consequently failure-free, is to be resisted at all costs. Failure is to be savoured and appreciated as both humorous and educational. There is nothing to be gained by such attempts at self-redemption. At the very least, all you have done is prove to the object of your affection how right they were in their decision to reject your advances.

The Pre-emptive Rejection
When asking someone out, a useful little trick I've learnt over the years is to get your own rejection in before the other person actually has a chance to reject you. It also helps if you ask the question in as vapid and vague a manner as possible, so that your intentions can be open to interpretation, should they be called into question.

"I was wondering, if you might possibly want to... I mean you don't have to… but, err, I thought I might ask whether you would like to… No, of course you wouldn't, I understand completely. What was I thinking?"

This way, you can leave the room with your dignity intact, having denied them the opportunity to embarrass you.

Dumping
Upon hearing the news that a friend's relationship has just ended, you are legally obliged to ask, "Who dumped who?" as your first question. Laws on this subject go back to the time of Henry VIII, who controversially executed Thomas More for asking that very question during the annulment of his marriage to Catherine of Aragon.

Dumping stamps the seal of failure onto the conclusion to a relationship. It can be a protracted and drawn out affair, sometimes taking months, years or even the death of one of the participants to expedite. One technique, usually but not exclusively employed by men, is to act in a feckless and indolent manner until such time as their girlfriends can no longer stand their behaviour. In this way, the relationship is brought to a close at the behest of the man, although it appears to be at the instigation of the woman. This state of affairs is, ironically, the opposite of what occurs at the start of relationships, where men think they are instigating something that women have actually already determined themselves.

One man's rejection is another man's (or woman's) lucky escape.

Final Thoughts

Love, like most things, is a two-sided coin. One man's rejection is another man's (or woman's) lucky escape. Your failure is someone else's success. You can, at the very worst, console yourself that you have saved some lucky individual and indeed yourself from a protracted and ill-matched relationship that is destined to end in tears. A well-timed rejection in the first ten minutes can save years of anguish on both sides. And think of the children. The importance of this cannot be overestimated, and should be considered of great comfort and solace in your time of needy desperation. It should also be noted that a great many successful relationships start out after one of more of the participants are feeling needy, desperate and full of self-loathing following a previous rejection.

CHAPTER 4
SPORT

Keep in mind that neither success nor failure is ever final.
Roger Babson

The sporting arena is the home turf of failure, for there can be no competition without at least one loser. On first inspection, it would seem quite easy to fail at sport. A regular diet of pies, chips, beer and cigarettes, combined with a sedentary lifestyle and a lack of hand-eye co-ordination make it child's play to perform with ineptitude at even the simplest physical activity. We should all therefore feel comfortable and familiar with losing at sport.

However, true sporting failure can only occur within the framework of willing participation. You may wish to be sociable with friends who favour a particular sport; or you may be living the sitcom cliché, with a boss who determines your future on a round of golf. You may simply be a glutton for punishment, who gets some kind of perverted thrill from being kicked around a pitch in the stead of a ball.

Bad Losers

They say that the notion of an English gentleman is one of a man gracious in defeat and generous in victory. Speaking on behalf of my nation, we have certainly had more practice at defeat than victory over the years, which may have helped to shape this character. Everyone likes to see a competitor calmly accept the result, shake the hand of their opponent, hand over their money and coolly walk away. But this can look like indifference – as if they didn't care, or weren't really trying. To give the impression that the contest is of immense personal importance, you have to be a bad loser. And while spectators applaud a good loser, they just can't get enough of the bad-boy sportsman who will never accept the prospect of defeat. This is the best, most showy response to your own failure, and, of course, the explanation for the popularity of tennis. Consequently, there are a number of ways in which you can manifest your disappointment.

The Sulk

There are few sights more self-indulgent than that of the sulk. To perfect the attitude, you must refuse to shake the hand of your opponent, throw down any equipment you might be holding, walk up and down purposefully whilst avoiding everyone's gaze, and finally sit in a corner, brooding, harbouring evil thoughts about the victor.

The Tantrum

A true classic. Screaming and shouting obscenities, you must deny the very fact of your loss. Blame everyone else – referees, umpires, spectators, team-mates – for the result. Break something. Pretend that you did, in fact, win. Stick your fingers in your ears and say "La la la, not listening, aaaah". Grab the trophy for which you are playing, and only relinquish it when they prise it from your cold, dead hands.

The Schoolboy

Every schoolboy knows that it is far better to destroy ones toys than to have to share them. And there are few more satisfying ways of losing badly than smashing or setting fire to the equipment and facilities of your chosen sport. That way, your failure will never again be repeated; and what is more, your conqueror will never relive his moment of glory against you or anyone else. In the immortal words of a US army lieutenant: "in order to save the village, we destroyed the village."

There's No "I" in Team

It's all very well and good coping with your own ineptitude, but when you play as part of a team, you will have to face the judgment and wrath of your team-mates when things go wrong. They were depending on you, and, quite frankly, you let them down. And, most importantly of all, as they will also tell you, you let yourself down. So, if you're happy about letting yourself down, you don't need to be too worried about letting them down. Eventually, either you or they will decide that you probably shouldn't play anymore. Trust me: it's for the best.

Excuses

These days, most professional sportsmen and women are taught how to comment upon their performance in television interviews. Behind the scenes, teams of writers are thinking up their best excuses for failure. You yourself may decide to shrug off your defeat as the product of some freak event, and produce any number of excuses for your risible performance:

- "I'm used to playing with different rules."

- "The pitch conditions just weren't right."

- "My opponent has the advantage of being left-handed."

- "I have the disadvantage of being left-handed."

- "The sun was in my eyes."

- "The referee must have had the sun in his eyes."

- "I was breaking in a new jockstrap."

- "I've been having personal problems at home."

- "I have a terrible hangover."

- "Those steroids have made my head go all funny."

Of course, what you should rather do is to laugh at your performance, and explain quite clearly that you lost because you are just really bad at sport.

Individual Sports

If you insist on participating in sports, you will need to know what it is you need to do in order to fail. This would seem to involve some understanding of the rules – and that would be too much like interest. So, to save you years of hardship, here are some popular sports and the chief methods of attaining your goal.

Tennis

The coup de grace in tennis is the ace, whereby one player serves the ball towards the other player, who is unable or unwilling to return the ball. Therefore, to fail at tennis, you simply have to stand there and do nothing. Your opponent will think himself a highly skilled competitor on the basis of your complete lack of movement. People who make such crass, self-aggrandising judgments are not worthy of your competition or your respect.

Cricket

Cricket is the sport of gentlemen, and, consequently, failure is essential and even encouraged. The fumbled catch, the wide ball and the sloppy stroke are all practised by even the best exponents of the game. If you can manage it, try to get out LBW, so that, in the post-match analysis in the bar, you can then claim that the umpire's decision was dodgy.

Soccer

There are many opportunities to fail in soccer. Kicking the ball wildly towards the goalmouth – yours or the oppositions – is a technique that will stand up to scrutiny as a valiant attempt that didn't quite come off. The pitfalls of the offside rule provide another chance to shine.

Rugby

Again, in rugby, standing still is the key to failure. However, with this strategy comes the certainty of injury, as players twice your body weight smash into you. Running away from the main area of play can be used to great effect, and many is the try that has been unwittingly scored by a winger who was just trying to escape from the field.

> *One of the most important lessons of failure is that when you compete against yourself, one of you will always lose.*

Golf

This sport has been described in many ways in the past, such as "glorified tidying-up", or "a good walk spoilt". But it still remains one of the easiest games to fail in a convincing way. Using antique equipment with inappropriate clothes is just the beginning. The rest is simply down to hand-eye co-ordination and technique. In golf, you do not so much compete against an opponent as much as you compete against yourself. One of the most important lessons of failure is that when you compete against yourself, one of you will always lose.

Spectating

One way of involving yourself in sport without the risk of failure is to spectate. Most spectators are happy to bask in the reflected glory of a successful team or individual, yet become strangely reticent when thing go wrong. Occasionally, a few die-hard fans will cry with sympathy for the failure of their team. This is a rare instance of other people's failure being treated with the same degree of emotion as your own. Such altruism should be rewarded with such comforting words as "it's only a game…"

Final Thoughts

It does occur to me that if chemicals which enhance your performance, such as steroids, are banned within professional sport, then surely chemicals which reduce your performance, such as alcohol and nicotine, should be encouraged, or at least afforded some weighted handicap. But apparently not.

The word "sport" covers a multitude of activities these days, but there are, as my grandfather used to say, only three sports: hunting, shooting, and fishing. All the rest are mere games and pastimes. And, if you are going to fail at these three sports, you only need to worry if you yourself are being hunted, shot at, or indeed fished. As for games and pastimes, my final word of advice is to play only those games at which it is impossible to lose, such as Naked Twister. If you're already playing, you're already winning.

CHAPTER 5
GREAT FAILURES
THROUGHOUT HISTORY

Sometimes a noble failure serves the world as
faithfully as a distinguished success.
Edward Dowden

Throughout our lives, we continually have the achievements of others thrust in our faces – particularly when we fail. This usually starts with your parents pointing out that someone else's child of about your age has achieved something that you haven't. It may well be the case that little Tommy Henderson next door knows how to tie his shoelaces; or is learning the piano; or doesn't get arrested for petty theft: but that doesn't really make him the benchmark for humanity, does it, mother? Next, of course, we see the school prizes, awarded to our peers for academic and sporting prowess; and so it goes on until finally we are shown the achievements of Leonardo da Vinci in comparison to own meagre efforts.

But when you're sitting on the stairs, in the darkness, crying into your gin, it's nice to remind yourself that some of the most illustrious achievers in recorded civilisation, whose lives and achievements you might look up to and aspire to, have also failed in one way or another. If they have failed too, why should anyone expect more than that of you? In fact, on the available evidence, people should expect quite a lot less of you than they do.

There are a great many great men who are revered for their works and yet died both unappreciated and penniless. And so, to comfort and console you in your despair, here's an irreverent look at some of the most brilliant and famous names in history.

Socrates (469–399 BC)

The Father of Philosophy, Socrates introduced many concepts to Western thinking, such as inductive and deductive reasoning. However, his method of constant questioning succeeded only to irritate everyone else, and he was condemned to death for inventing the child's game of continually asking "why?". Given the opportunity to commit suicide, he couldn't even do that properly, taking some 48 hours to die by hemlock poisoning. By the second day, you would think that he would have tried a couple of other methods, just to be on the safe side.

Alexander the Great (356–323 BC)

This Macedonian prince forged an empire from his homelands to the Hindu Kush in India. We are told that "when Alexander saw the breadth of his domain, he wept: for there were no more worlds to conquer". So it appears that Alexander was at least a failure in his own eyes. And, whilst most of us have not forged an empire spanning the best part of known civilisation, a significant number of us manage to avoid dying in Babylon at the age of 34.

Michelangelo Buonarroti (1475–1564)

This Italian polymath achieved so much as a painter, sculptor and architect that it is almost impossible to think how he might be considered a failure. Well, it may seem a footling thing to do, but we should judge the man by his own high standards. Firstly, he wrote some poetry which is either second-rate or unfairly overshadowed by the light of his other accomplishments, depending upon your point of view. Secondly, he spent the last twelve years of his life trying unsuccessfully to finish the Pietá Rondanini sculpture, and still couldn't do the hands. (They are always the trickiest bit, as any artist will tell you.)

George Frederick Handel (1685–1759)

Handel was, in his own words, an Englishman "by choice". However, he was rather hampered in this regard by being German by birth. Inspired by the great music of Johann Sebastian Bach, he wrote many fine musical works, hoping to promote music within England, which the Germans at that time called "the land without music". By composing Oratorios, such as The Messiah, he accidentally invented the choral society, and so he is ultimately responsible for a vast amount of bad singing and regular displays of musical ineptitude up and down the land.

Doctor Joseph Ignace Guillotin (1738–1814)

The inventor of the guillotine was, ironically, opposed to the death penalty. Something of a snob, he pragmatically argued that if people must be executed, then at least the aristocracy should be despatched in as humane and painless a way as possible. The lower classes, however, were to remain subject to the more usual, mediaeval methods of punishment. The French Revolution saw not only a huge increase in state-sanctioned death sentences, but also an egalitarian edict that all those condemned should die by the same means – his invention.

Jeremy Bentham (1748–1832)

English philosopher who stated that all rational activity is based on the fundamental desire to seek pleasure and avoid pain. His life's work is belied by the fact that his embalmed corpse is regularly invited to dinner engagements – and what is more, attends. Neither Bentham nor his hosts can gain much pleasure or avoid much pain by this activity, performed by otherwise rational people. Thus, Bentham's own body disproves his own philosophical theory, silently and surreally, for eternity.

Sir Alexander Fleming (1844–1955)

A great leading light of Microbiology, who worked to promote health and cleanliness, and to reduce the risk of infection. To his perpetual shame, he is best known for not tidying his work away, so that it went mouldy overnight.

Bertrand Russell (1872–1970)

One of the greatest intellects of recent times, Russell spent a lifetime acquiring a huge understanding of logic and mathematics in order to solve problems, only to prove conclusively that there are some problems which cannot be solved by logic and mathematics. QED.

Aleister Crowley (1875–1947)

At one time considered "the most evil man in the world", this twentieth-century magician performed rituals, such as the Goetia, in order to make Faustian pacts with the Devil. He died penniless in a run-down Bed & Breakfast on Brighton sea-front at the age of 72 after years of ill-health. If you are going to sell your soul to Satan, it's always a good idea to get the cash, women and long-life up front.

William "Bill" Gates (1955–present)

Possibly the richest man on the planet, Bill Gates has created the most powerful and dominant computer software company, amassing billions of dollars for both himself and his business. It seems strange then, that with practically unlimited resources available to him, he still cannot make an operating system that is stable, secure, efficient or user-friendly.

CHAPTER 6
EDUCATION

Three failures denote uncommon strength.
A weakling has not enough grit to fail thrice.
Minna Thomas Antrim

School is where we first learn a multitude of social failure. It is not clear why, amongst so many failings that we experience at school, someone saw fit to add to these the prospect of academic failure. It is a rare child indeed that does not fail well in at least one academic discipline: and if such a child does exist, it will certainly be frail and unsuited to the physical elements of the curriculum. This dichotomy is, of course, the original realisation of our doomed existence to failure. School is where we are first introduced to areas of human endeavour that our outside our particular strengths and abilities. As a result, the one thing you can be sure to learn at school is how to fail.

Most of us fall somewhere in the middle-ground between numbingly stupid and irritatingly bright, perhaps excelling in one subject area and failing hideously in another. Some of us cannot grasp the rigidity of Sciences; others are nonplussed by the vagaries of the Humanities. And so, as a compromise between these two fields, the Social Sciences were born, as a kind of grey area in which any student, no matter what their particular bent, can be expected to perform to a mediocre level. Despite these intentions, many students continue to make heavy weather of even these subjects.

Education is divided into two main events: the prolonged, tedious, interminable agony of daily learning; and the panicky, fleeting zenith of examination, the means by which our learning is tested. And so we must all endure these same petty agonies, and learn how to fail both the annual round of examination and the daily grind of schooling.

In recent years, educators have argued that testing a year's learning on one given day might possibly be deeply unfair, suggesting that nothing could be worse than having your future development decided by the assessment of your performance on one day of the year. As an alternative, educational scientists have worked out that something indeed might be worse, and they named it continual assessment. In this approach, your yearly examination is broken down into small, weekly pieces that you can fail in a more manageable way. Whilst you might easily argue that on the day of an exam you were having an "off" day, it is a bit more difficult to maintain that you had an "off" year, or indeed, an "off" life.

Exams

Examinations are to many the yardstick by which our failure is measured. Much pressure is often put upon students, increasing the panicked certainty of failure. These pressures can be triggered by such seemingly innocuous factors as the exam hall itself. Exams are often held in the school's sports hall, simply because it is the largest empty room that the school possesses. To a moody, hormonal adolescent, there can be few things more guaranteed to promote a tense, sexually-charged atmosphere in which serious academic rigour is impossible than the enforced silence of a pheromone-filled gymnasium in the height of summer. There can be no greater distraction and spur to failure. An alternative to the gymnasium, if the school is grand enough, is a purpose-built assembly room or hall, usually filled with lists of successful candidates from previous years, who sat the very same exam that you are now sitting. Surely flaunting the success of others in front of you only serves to make matters worse. The only other place that exams are located is a library, where the books containing the answers are tantalisingly just out of reach. It is strange that educators do not seem to give any of these facts due consideration when selecting the venue for examinations.

Even in such seemingly austere surroundings, the potential for distraction is rife. First is the almost neurotic compulsion to order one's pencils, pens, chewing gum and lucky charms by size, or make them form geometric patterns aligned to the edges of the desk. Next comes the vacuous staring at a fixed point in the distance, or some architectural appreciation of the hall. Eventually, you must turn your attention to the dauntingly grim task of putting pen to paper, and answering the questions on the exam paper.

There are three common types of exam: multiple choice, essay and oral. We will look at each of these types, and discuss how best to manifest failure. (As if advice were needed.)

Multiple choice

Multiple choice questions are those for which only one of a number of provided answers is correct. The candidates must, using their skill and judgment, select whichever they believe to be the true answer. For this reason, it is sometimes known as "multi-guess", as a blind stab-in-the-dark is often as good as a considered, reasoned response. Teachers will often encourage their pupils afterwards by telling them that their score was statistically lower than that which a monkey, selecting answers at random, should get.

Assuming a lack of knowledge of the subject matter, there are a number of different strategies open to the canny student:

- All Bs – the answers are usually labelled alphabetically. At the start of the exam, choose one letter, and select that answer for every question. It is imperative that you do not waver from your choice, even if you think the answer you have selected is quite clearly wrong.

- Join the Dots – the answers are submitted on a special form, allowing you to create a pattern of your choice using a purely artistic or geometric criterion. This gives the impression of your having duly weighed each option before selecting one, and is not so immediately obvious to the assessor as the "All Bs" strategy.

- Random Factor – your answers are selected purely at random. You can either summon psychic energy to gauge the answer without even looking at the question, or you may roll a die. (6 means "roll again".) If you don't have a die, you can use the hexagonal surfaces of a pencil as a makeshift random number generator.

- Blind Fury – the final option available to candidates in multi-guess exams is to demand an answer that is not catered for. Each of the available options does not match your own assessment of the question, and all of them seem equally worthless. Write a small essay on some spare note-paper, indicating why your choice is correct, and work yourself up into a fury at the short-sightedness of the examiners for not including it. Finally, remember to "spoil" your answer sheet, in a futile attempt to select an answer which transcends the design of the sheet.

Essay answers

Essays have to be written in two distinct ways. In Science papers, you must use your knowledge and reasoning to come up with the prescribed answer. In Humanities, you may come up with any old answer, as long as you have used your reasoning and knowledge. The difference between these two approaches is indicative of the differences between Arts and Sciences. Apart from these conditions, the rest is up to you. Here, verbal diarrhoea or free word association are both winning tactics – and this is probably the only time in your life when this will be true.

It would seem quite easy to fail, simply by ensuring that your essay is relatively content-free, with spurious reasoning, outmoded arguments, and incorrect assertions. However, the majority of essays are marked in a subjective way, so that the same techniques that ought to guarantee failure might actually prove successful. The provision of facts or examples with which the examiner is unfamiliar might be credited with points, if he cannot be bothered to check them. My old Geography teacher used to assure me that the town of Merthyr Tydfil, in Wales, was the perfect instance of every geological, topographical and demographical observation that you might care to mention. I have never been to the town, so cannot dispute whether, for example, it might be an archipelago that displays U-shaped glacial valleys and whose population forms an inverted bell demographic graph.

Some essays are required to be of a minimum word length. In order to achieve the required word count, it is very important to use padding, such as "in fact", "it is rather interesting to note that", "surprisingly", and other spurious phrases that add no actual content to the sentence. It is rather interesting to note that, surprisingly, the amount of extra padding in a sentence can in fact increase its length by up to 38%. This will not help, however, if points are also being awarded for literary style.

Oral examinations

As an alternative to failing a written exam, where your thought processes and errors can be shown to the world as a permanent record of failure, there is the oral exam. The oral exam rarely succeeds in being taken seriously, because schoolboys can't say the word 'oral' without giggling. In such an exam, you are expected to think spontaneously, and come up with answers in real time. At least in a written exam, you can throw away the piece of paper with your first answer, and no-one will be any the wiser. And you can always doodle if bored. In an oral exam, verbal doodling is not recommended as a technique for whiling the time away.

Oral exams are often set to determine a candidate's ability in a foreign language. This adds another dimension of failure to the proceedings. You not only have to worry about what you might find yourself saying, but also your ability to say it. In such circumstances, it is quite easy to wander off into areas where your vocabulary might let you down, such as architecture, parapsychology, cheese manufacturing processes, or, in my own case, the plots of science fiction films of the 1980s. Your best course of action would be to keep the conversation as bland and pointless as the vocabulary you have learned.

Cheating

Much social stigma is placed upon cheating. Or at least, getting caught cheating. This comes from the erroneous assumption that everyone is on what is referred to as a "level playing-field", and that those who cheat give themselves an unfair advantage. But surely, the more intelligent children have an unfair advantage over the less intelligent. The diligent over the work-shy. Or are they fair advantages? Surely, the cheat does nothing more than create a fair advantage for himself, according to his particular talents.

It is not clear whether cheating constitutes failure or not. Certainly, being caught cheating is a failure, and can be dealt with quite harshly, depending upon the environment in which it occurs.

You may find yourself pilloried by those who were playing by the rules. You may be expelled from the school or professional body that organised the exam. Only very rarely might you be commended for your display of initiative.

IQ Tests

Occasionally, at school and elsewhere, we may be invited to take an IQ test. This usually involves pattern recognition within a sequence of numbers, words, or shapes. However, any IQ test is only as accurate as the IQ of the person who set it. It may be that someone of a vastly superior intellect can spot an equally valid, but different answer from the supposedly correct one. In theory then, a genius may perform poorly in such a test. Well, that's my excuse anyway, and I'm sticking to it.

It is a well-proven fact that people at the very top end of the IQ scale do not actually perform as well in the real world as they do in IQ tests.

> *Teachers are traditionally the instruments of failure in all good educational establishments.*

Failure in the Classroom

If exams are the milestones along the path of failure, then the day-to-day trials and tribulations of the classroom are the footfalls. Teachers are traditionally the instruments of failure in all good educational establishments. They are the mechanism both by which we fail to learn, and by which our failure is discovered. They themselves can fail, depending upon their own personal goals, in their attempts to impart both their wisdom and a sense of discipline or self-worth to their students.

It is amazing how quickly students can learn if properly motivated. For instance, most students will start their academic careers by answering any questions put to the class by the teacher. They will continue answering questions until such time as either their classmates pillory them for being the teacher's pet, or the teacher humiliates them in front of their peers for supplying an incorrect answer. After that, the child has successfully learnt not to answer the teacher's questions if he can possibly avoid it. This is how conventional schooling has worked for hundreds of years.

It is sometimes claimed that the brightest students are often those who show little interest in their lessons. They can be unruly and ill-disciplined, it is said, failing tests in an effort to relieve the boredom of the teaching. This would appear to be a rare example of society accepting failure in a more compassionate and responsive way than usual. However, in fairness, it is probably only mothers who say this sort of thing.

Final Thoughts

You never stop learning, it is said. But institutional education, as a playground of failure, is where we first learn the many different ways we can fail. As we progress up the educational ladder, we are told to choose progressively fewer subjects to study. However, from the point of view of failure, you are not actively choosing subjects, but rather dropping those at which you have displayed a particular incompetence. This leaves you with a small area of knowledge in which you can display average levels of competence, or at least bluff your way through.

CHAPTER 7
HOPE, LUCK AND FAILURE – THE RATIONAL MODEL

Not many people are willing to give failure a second opportunity.
Joseph Sugarman

Hope, luck and failure are intricately interrelated. We hope for a particular outcome, luck conspires against us, and consequently, we fail. These things, which are possibly three of the most important factors of our lives, need and deserve to be carefully studied, rigorously analysed, poked and prodded in a pseudo-scientific manner. What then are these things called hope, luck and failure?

Hope

As a wise man once said, hope is a bastard. Hope is the expectation of things that reality and experience should have taught us will never happen. It is the triumph of naivety over wisdom. Perversely, the further we progress on the path of failure, the more we hope for the success that eludes us. This explain why gamblers will keep putting their chips on black, even though the roulette wheel has come up red the last forty times. The gambler will believe that the more often the ball lands on red, the more likely the chance that it will land on black the next time. A more dispassionate soul might simply suggest that the wheel was fixed.

Luck

Some people believe that we are the play-things of the Gods. They toy with us for their sport. Others maintain that it is merely the random, chaotic factors of chance that produce such bitter-sweet ironies from day to day. Whichever one you choose to believe, you will certainly speak of your luck, be it good or bad. Our failure, in our own eyes, will depend upon our luck.

Luck is therefore just a measure of how much the actualities of life conform to our desires or expectations. If things turn out as we wished, or better, we say we are lucky. If things turn out worse than we would wish, we say we are unlucky. It was pure luck, we say, that the woman I mortally offended at a party last week is now interviewing me for a job. It is only my bad luck that prevents me from winning the lottery every week. The fact that a pigeon has just crapped on me is, I am told, a sign of remarkable good fortune, although I myself cannot quite see how this fits into the theory.

Failure

If failure needs any introduction at this stage of the book, then I have certainly met with it.

Risible Maths

It now remains to show exactly how hope, luck and failure interact with each other, in a clearly defined, mathematical way. Using a minimal command of algebra and Cartesian geometry, and guided by a half-hearted scientific rigour, I hope to form conclusions about the interaction of these three elements of human existence. This will, I hope, bring us comfort and a greater understanding of the human condition. I should perhaps warn those of you who particularly fail in the field of mathematics, that there will be both equations and graphs in what follows. However, they can easily be ignored, and they are subordinate to the conclusions that they provide.

Any given activity will require a level of difficulty within a certain range. Whether you fail at it, or not, depends upon your particular ability, the level of difficulty you are attempting, and blind luck. This can be represented by the following graph:

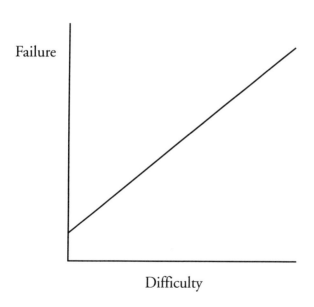

You can see that as the level of difficulty increases, the likelihood of your failing also increases. The steepness of the increase is inversely proportional to your ability. In other words, a more able person's failure will not be as great as a less able person's, for the same level of difficulty. Good luck reduces the size of the failure, and bad luck increases it. Note that on this graph, even a task with a difficulty level of zero still comes with some inherent risk of failure. This is a very important lesson to learn.

Therefore, from the graph, we can produce the equation:

$$F = D/A - L$$

where **F** equals failure, **D** is the level of difficulty, **A** is your ability, and **L** is luck, (bad luck being a negative value and good luck being positive).

Producing an expression for luck we come up with:

$$L = D/A - F$$

All this simply serves to show that luck is nothing more than an assessment of an event's outcome, given our particular abilities. In other words, good luck is an outcome that is better than expected, and bad luck is an outcome that is worse than expected.

But of what of your hopes and dreams? How do they fit in? Hope is a prediction of the outcome of a situation, multiplied out of all proportion by the unrealistic factor, **U**.

Hope can be represented thus:

$$H = U. A/D$$

This gives us the following graph.

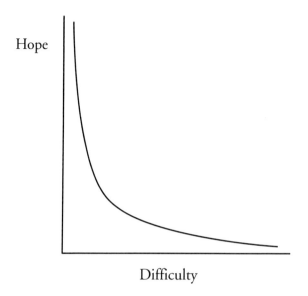

Hope

Difficulty

Note here that as the difficulty increases, there is always a positive amount of hope, even at an infinite level of difficulty. At the other end of the graph, maximum levels of hope occur as difficulty approaches zero. However, the graph also shows that difficulty never reaches zero, and thus every activity does require some element of skill.

Because the terms **A** and **D** feature in each equation, we can combine the two equations to create a new one, relating hope and failure.

$$H = U/(F + L)$$

Hope is therefore an unrealistic assessment of the world, offset by luck and failure. The term (F+L) might possible be called the cynicism factor.

Rearranging the same equation for failure, we get:

$$F = U/(H - L)$$

This equation gives us a similarly shaped graph, which shows the relationship between hope and failure.

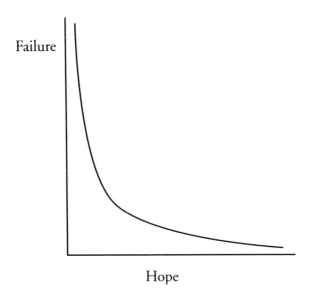

This clearly shows that hope never dies. As failure ascends to near infinite levels, we still believe, against all reason, that we can succeed. This is sheer human folly. This is why hope is such a terrible blight upon our lives, as it belies the inevitable prospect of failure. Similarly, at the other end of the graph, where hope is at its highest, the possibility of failure dwindles, but is always there. Failure, too, it would seem, never dies.

This last equation clearly shows that failure is the product of three factors: hope, luck, and an unrealistic assessment of your abilities. All of these three things are in your mind. Therefore, failure is nothing more than a figment of your own overactive and bewildered imagination. Consequently, it should be treated in much the same way as hallucinations, jealousy or any other mental aberration. Who knows – in the future, it may even be possible to eradicate failure using advanced pharmacology. Chemists could sell you a blister pack of pills that will remove any trace of failure from your blighted life. This would, however, deprive you of the amusement that failure brings, so, like failure itself, is something of a mixed blessing.

Conclusion

With a minimal command of algebra and Cartesian geometry, I have proved beyond any doubt that hope does indeed spring eternal, and that luck and failure are simply products of our own imagination. These are all quite significant discoveries, and it remains to be seen how the scientific and philosophic communities will react to this ground-breaking news.

CHAPTER 8
OTHER ARENAS OF FAILURE

There's no greater success than failure.
Bob Dylan

General Life Skills

Of course, most of our failures do not occur on the grand stage, but are usually much more mundane, everyday and ordinary. However, it is this succession of seemingly insignificant failures that wears us down eventually, like a drop of water eroding granite across the millennia. How many of us have found ourselves struggling with the most basic of tasks that involve the minimum level of hand-eye co-ordination? Last year, seven hundred and twenty four people died as a direct result of injuries sustained whilst attempting to put their socks on.

Statistically, the home is the most dangerous place, and you are lucky to get out of it alive each morning. So you should count your blessings, and take pride in even this simple achievement. Every day, otherwise normal, competent people stab themselves in the eye with a fork, stick their fingers into food processors, or drink a tall glass of bleach and tonic with ice and a slice. The number of injuries sustained from falling pianos, safes and anvils would suggest that we are all running around like Tom and Jerry. (Watch out for that garden rake, by the way.) Failure is everywhere, all around us, and it cannot be avoided.

Drink

With drink often comes embarrassment, and there are few things worse than being the most drunk in the room. Except being the most sober person in the room, obviously. Alcohol is very often the lubrication on which the wheels of failure spin. It has two main effects that promote failure. Firstly, it reduces co-ordination and motor skills. Secondly, it removes that part of your brain function that says "it's probably best if it you didn't do that". To match these two properties, it has two redeeming features. It casts a cloud over your memory, obscuring from your mind the ridiculous nature of your failings, until some well-meaning soul explains to you exactly what it was that his mother found so objectionable. Alcohol also offers its own mitigation. Many people believe that their own behaviour can be excused, simply by saying "Oh, well, I was drunk", or "it was just the beer talking". However, this is another deplorable instance of shifting blame away from yourself to something less tangible. What you should do is accept the blame, accept your fundamental flaws, and see the humour therein.

The Romans realised that *in vino veritas* – in wine, there is truth. And if they can accept the fallibility of man after he's had a few, and still go on to conquer most of the known world, then why should we be any different? But then the Romans didn't conquer the world with comedy. They used big swords.

Professional Failings

Each career, profession and trade brings with it its own unique, inherent opportunities to fail. It would seem prudent to reflect on them, before – or indeed after – considering a career in that particular area.

Medicine

Medicine, as any doctor facing charges of negligence will tell you, is not an exact science. The consequences of failure in this field tend to have rather a ring of permanency to them. And yet, strange as it may seem, doctors too are only human.

Whenever you hear a doctor say to you "Oh, sorry, was I supposed to remove the left kidney...?" you should think about the failures that you make in your place of work, and be grateful that the consequences of your blunders are likely to be significantly less important. In many careers, turning up in the morning with a hangover is acceptable – and in some cases obligatory. Why then should we treat doctors any differently?

Science

Science is a discipline in which you would think failure had little place. However, like all human endeavours, it is not only riddled with failure, but it also depends upon a certain amount of the stuff, too. A great many discoveries and inventions, such as rocket science or the cure for leprosy, came about whilst failing to achieve something quite different and usually much more inconsequential, like trying to stop fresh bread from breaking when you spread cold butter on it. Many of the brave pioneers on the cutting edge of scientific endeavour only found out what they had achieved once their hangover had settled.

As any good scientist (or any mediocre one for that matter) will tell you, an experiment is only a failure if you learn nothing from it. So, the more a scientist fails, the wiser he ought to be. Unless he is very stupid, of course.

Engineering

Here is one area of endeavour where failure plays an important – nay, vital – role. For instance, more has been learnt about aircraft design from the planes that killed test pilots than from the ones whose pilots walked away safely. Would we know as much about vortices in air currents, had the Tacoma bridge not wobbled itself to destruction in the 1940s? Would we care so much about air currents, if someone hadn't built a wobbly bridge?

Showbusiness

There are two main categories of failure in showbusiness. First is the rather subjective failing of being not very skilled in your particular métier, such as acting, singing or dancing; and second is the more definitive failure involved in producing a spectacle that loses money at the box-office. Each, of course, blames the other for its failings. Of course, you can always dismiss the critics who dismiss your labours. Casting directors who do not book you are obviously biased, incompetent, or lacking in vision. However, losing millions by not getting bums on seats is a more tangible failure, and one that is not easily hidden. Luckily, it is an accepted business model that the Arts are not expected to make money. This mitigates the failure simply by not considering profit as an objective. As the jazz club owner Ronnie Scott used to say: it's easy to make a million from a jazz club. Start with two million.

Fine Art

In some perverse fields of endeavour, acts of failure are seen as a brand of success. Many artists see success, in a conventional sense, as "selling-out", and incompatible with remaining true to one's art. Like their heroes, such people would prefer to die unappreciated and penniless, as it keeps their art sharp, fresh and visceral. Again, this shows the subjective, transcendental quality of failure, where some people actually prefer it and seek after it.

Religion

Many religions have something to say on the subject of failure. Most tend to be against it. But nearly all of them suggest that you should strive in an unrealistic way, contrary to human nature, towards an unattainable goal that will inevitably involve failing when you try. This would seem to be a denial of our humanity, and doesn't really help the situation by adding to the list of things that we are not allowed to do. By creating these proscriptions, religions only increase the likelihood of our failure, and encourage an attitude of shame and embarrassment. Only Zen Buddhism offers a humorous approach to achievement and failure alike, but it does this through a series of surreal jokes, known as koans, which aren't actually that funny, even when you have attained enlightenment.

Politics

Having achieved the initial success of being voted into office, politics is one of the few areas in life where your success or failure seems to have little or no impact upon your career. Many is the politician who has displayed frightening ineptitude, incompetence or indifference, and yet has continued in office, been promoted, or otherwise rewarded. It is perhaps for this reason that so many people with a rare talent for failure seek out a career in this particular arena.

Final Thoughts

Every different walk of life brings with it its own peculiar opportunities to fail. Be prepared to jump right in.

CHAPTER 8
CONCLUSION

No more be grieved at that which thou has done.
Sonnet 35, William Shakespeare

We have, I hope, learnt that there is no shame in failure. To fail is, after all, only human – and there is only a small degree of shame in being human, and in that we all take an equal share. All of us fail, and all of us do so in often spectacular ways. If we are to make any sense of this meaningless circle of existence, we must appreciate our humanity, warts and all – and that includes failure. Failure is an opportunity to learn; but above all, it is an opportunity to laugh. We should not be scared to fail, any more than we should be scared to succeed. Success and failure are but two sides of the same coin.

Laughter reconciles us to our frailty, reveals our foolish pride, and reduces us to a humble, but happy state. It is therefore the best remedy for all our errors, failings, misadventures and mistakes. Laughing at your own failure encourages others to laugh at it too, and laughter is the best forgiveness.

It has become clear that the majority of failure is simply a result of our own over-blown expectations and aspirations. It takes nothing more than a change of outlook to re-appraise our shortcomings and realise that failure is an integral part of our make-up – one which we cannot do without.

So, the next time you consider yourself to have failed, take a moment to think. Might there be any humour in the risibility of your performance? Did you achieve a new personal best in ineptitude? Did you say exactly the wrong thing to someone important? Did you fall over and land in the buffet? The best way to raise yourself from your self-imposed shame and despair is to laugh and to realise that you are just like the rest of us.

ABOUT THE AUTHOR

Rarely is an author so well-informed about his subject. Ben Byram-Wigfield has been seeking out failure since he attempted to make his first footsteps as an infant, and it's all gone downhill from there. Despite supposed advantages of education and breeding, he has managed to avoid fulfilling any potential he may once have had. He has never got a job from an interview in the face of competition. Having tried his hand at any number of different careers – musician, scientist, teacher, computer programmer, administrator, salesman, impresario, turf accountant, shoe consultant and pub landlord – he has come to the rather inevitable conclusion that he is not really cut out for work. Like many others of a feckless, indolent and work-shy nature, he has decided to take up writing, and looks forward to failing in this new field of endeavour. His parents are strangely proud of him, believing him to be "just a late developer, that's all". They are, however, currently taking legal advice about reclaiming the money they spent on all those schools.

His hobbies include mooching, shirking and a daily lounge. He lives in Seclusion, a small town in the West Midlands.